CW00816408

The Fall Of Poland In 1794
Tragic Drama, In Four Acts

A Patriot

THE

FALL OF POLAND

In 1794:

AN

HISTORICAL TRAGIC DRAMA,

IN FOUR ACTS.

BY

A PATRIOT.

" But *all are Slaves; whereas* by Nature's laws
Fair LIBERTY's the BIRTHRIGHT of Mankind!"

Page 53.

Malone Æt. 35.

LONDON:

LONGMAN, BROWN, GREEN, AND LONGMANS.

1855.

Dedication.

TO

THE TRUE FRIENDS AND PROMOTERS OF

LIBERTY

THROUGHOUT

BRITANNIA, GALLIA, HIBERNIA, AND SCOTIA,

THE

TRAGIC DRAMA

OF

" The Fall of Poland "

IS INSCRIBED,

IN THE HOPE OF ITS BEING IN SOME WAY INSTRUMENTAL IN AROUSING
AN ACTIVE, ENERGETIC, AND SUCCESSFUL MOVEMENT

ON BEHALF OF

POLISH NATIONALITY,

WHEREBY THAT LONG OPPRESSED COUNTRY MAY,
AT NO DISTANT PERIOD,
BE RELEASED FROM THE GALLING CHAINS OF RUSSIAN DESPOTISM;

AND

BY THE FIRM BOND OF YOUR UNITED STRENGTH, DEVOTED
AND ENTHUSIASTIC ZEAL,

THAT POLAND MAY BE RAISED UP FROM HER LOW AND PROSTRATE
STATE, BASED ON THE FIRM AND TOWERING STRUCTURE OF LONG
AND LASTING FREEDOM, TILL SHE ASCENDS TRIUMPHANT IN HER
SOVEREIGN MIGHT

> " *To the bright Pinnacle of Liberty,—*
> *An Ornament to Nations, bless'd on Earth,*
> *While water'd with the dews from Heav'n above.*"—Kos. page 30.

IN THIS ARDENT AND SINCERE HOPE,

THE OFFERING OF A SYMPATHETIC HEART,

THE AUTHOR BEGS MOST UNFEIGNEDLY TO SUBSCRIBE HIMSELF,

YOUR MOST SINCERELY ATTACHED, DEVOTED,
AND FAITHFUL BROTHER,

A PATRIOT.

REMARKS.

In placing the Drama of "THE FALL OF POLAND" before the notice of the true friends and promoters of Liberty, the Author deems it of importance, at this particular period of the World's History, to give an HISTORICAL EPITOME, tracing out the rapid strides of *Russian aggression*, interspersed with some general REMARKS that may not be without their utility.

When we cast our eyes back to the close of the Seventeenth Century, we there behold the rise of one of those reigning monsters of iniquity in the person, style, and description of " Peter the Great, Czar or Emperor of Russia," " Father of his Country!" &c. &c. and such like profaned titles. We see in this Personage that ever-restless and untameable spirit of brute-force policy exerted against the liberties of mankind, whether in European or Asiatic States, the fruits of which we now behold so manifest in the present day, engendering in our minds serious apprehensions for the future!

It was after the capture of Azof (1), in 1695, that the covetous desires and malign propensities of this Monarch looked forward to the conquest of the Crimea (2), and thereby to facilitate his access to the East. We find that by the peace of Carlowitz (3), in 1699, this turbulent spirit was diverted for a time against the Turkish Empire, when he turned his rapacious glance in a northern direction towards

---

(1) Azov or Azof, Tanais, a Town and Fort of Russia, at the entrance of the Don, Sea of Azof, 25 m. E. of Taganrog. The Sea of Azov lies between lat. 45° 20′ and 47° 18′ N. and lon. 35° and 39° E.N.E. of the Black Sea, and connected therewith by the Strait of Yenikale.

(2) Crimea, Taurica Chersonesus, a Peninsula of S. Russia, formed by the Sea of Azov and the Black Sea.

(3) Carlowitz, Karlowitz, or Carlovitz, a Town of the Austrian Empire, Slavonian territory, and 8 m. S.S.E. Peterwardien.

the Baltic (1). From the ill-success of Peter at the first siege of
Narva (2), against that remarkable man Charles XII. of Sweden, we
find him successful at the battle of Dorpat (3), although insignificant
in itself, but from which we may reckon the data of Muscovite
warfare. The sieges of Marienbourg (4) and Notebourg soon followed
in the train of Peter's conquests ; as also that of Meinchantz, in
1703. From this period Russia held possession of a Baltic Port·
It was then that Peter, elated by his conquests, formed the project
of building a City, when St. Petersburg (5) was founded. In order
to protect this after-capital of Russia, the far-seeing eye of Peter, in
the winter of 1703, commenced that now formidable barrier to invasion—the town and fort of Cronstadt (6). After having obtained
a victory over the Swedes at Carelia, he directed his rapacious glance
for the second time towards Narva ; and by a wily stratagem in no
way redounding to the credit or earning the name of skilful General-
ship, but by one of those *treacherous* devices so common with
Muscovite barbarism, obtained possession of that devoted place in
1704. Another project of great moment to the Russian Empire
was commenced about this period, when a canal was formed which
united the rivers Msta (7) and Tvertza (8), thereby forming an un-
broken communication between the Caspian (9) and the Baltic Seas.

---

(1) Baltic, or East Sea, Mare Balticum, an extensive Sea of N. Europe,
enclosed by Sweden, Russia, Prussia, Mecklenbourg, and Denmark. Area,
including the Gulf of Bothnia, 125,000 square miles.
(2) Narva, a fortified river-Port Town of Russia, 81 m. W.S.W. St. Petersburg, on the Narova, 9 m. from its mouth in the Gulf of Finland. It consists
of an Old and New Town.
(3) Dorpat, or Derpt (Russian, Juriev), a Town of Russia, gov. Livonia, on
the Embach, 150 m. N.E Riga.
(4) Marienbourg (Lettish, Allohksne), a Town of Russia, gov. Livonia, on
the lake of same name, 57 m. S.W. Pskov.
(5) St. Petersburg, the modern Cap. City of the Russian Empire, on the
Neva Gulf of Finland, 20 m. E. Cronstadt. Lat. 59° 56′ 5″ N., lon. 30° 19′ E.
Pop. 500,000.
(6) Cronstadt or Kronstadt, a fortified Town of Russia, 18 m. W. St. Petersburg, of which it forms the Port. Lat. 59° 59′ 46″ N., lon. 29° 40′ 38″ E. Its
vast Port, the most important of the Russian marine, is divided into Three
Parts:—that on the E. is the Military Port, containing the Russian Fleet;
the Middle Port, used for refitting ships of war; and that on the W., for the
lading and discharging of large merchant vessels unable to reach St. Petersburg. The Forts strongly defended by Ramparts and Bastions.
(7) Msta, a River of Russia, govs. Iver and Novgorod ; after a N. and W.
course of 250 m. to Voltchok, a canal proceeds to connect it with the
(8) Tvertza, a River of Russia, gov. Tver ; after a S.E. course of 110 m.
joins the Volga, where a canal joins it with the Msta.
(9) Caspian Sea (Mare Hyrcanum), an inland Sea of W. Asia, between lat.
36° 40′ and 47° 20′ N., and lon. 46° 50′ and 54° 10′ E. ; enclosed by Russia,
Persia, &c. Length N. to S. about 700 m.

From an innate obstinate pride of Charles XII. and the utter disregard and contempt in which he held the growing military character of Russia, and his intermeddling with the internal disputes of Poland, are to be attributed the many losses (although brilliant in victory for a time) that King and the Swedish nation sustained. From the *forced election* of Augustus II. (the Elector of Saxony) (1) as King of Poland, in 1697, in opposition to that of Prince Conti, one of the most popular of the candidates for the Polish Crown, we may trace the first link in that long and heavy chain of *black* events which was to seize and grasp around with iron clutch the fair form of POLISH LIBERTY and chain her to the dust! " Since this period," says *Rulhière*, " Poland has always received her Kings under the *compulsion of foreign arms !*"

Peter and Charles separately espoused the cause of Prince Conti ; but Augustus, with his Saxon army (so hated by the Poles as mercenary intruders), felt confidence in being able to fight his own battles. The recovery of Livonia (2) from the Swedes, which was ceded by the Treaty of Oliva (3) on the 3rd of May, 1660, was one of his most anxious cares ; but his first attempt proving abortive, he called to his aid the Monster of Russia, who through avarice, and having his eye (for maritime purposes) on Ingria (4), the north-east part of Livonia, was not long in joining Augustus against Charles. The Swedes routed Augustus and his Saxons on the banks of the Dwina (5). Charles took Warsaw (6), and gained the Battle of Klissow, when Augustus fled to Cracow (7). Charles XII. crowned Stanislas Leszczynski King of Poland.

---

(1) Saxony (German, Sachsen), a Kingdom of Central Europe, in the middle of Germany, between lat. 50° 10′ and 51° 28′ N., and lon. 11° 55′ and 15° 3′ E.
(2) Livonia (Germ. Livland, or Liefland), a marit. gov. of Russia, between lat. 50° 30′ and 56° 20′ N., and lon. 24° and 28° E. Area, 20,450 sq. m. Riga the Capital.
(3) Oliva, a Village of W. Prussia, 5 m. N.W. Dantzig.
(4) Ingria (German, Ingermannland), a Prov. Russia, forming part of the gov. St. Petersburg.
(5) Dwina, Dvina, or Northern Dwina, an important River of Russia, govs. Vologda and Archangel, flows N.W. and enters the White Sea 20 m. below Archangel. Total course, 330 m.
(6) Warsaw (Pol. Warszawa, Germ. Warschau, Fren. Varsovie), Cap. of the Kingdom of Poland, on the Vistula. Lat. 52° 13′ 5″ N., lon. 21° 2′ 9″ E. Warsaw succeeded Cracow as the Cap. of Poland in 1566.
(7) Cracow (Ger. and Pol. Krakau), a City and ancient Cap. of Poland, lat. 50° 3′ 59″ N., lon. 19° 51′ 50″ E., on the Vistula.

Augustus, again defeated by Charles at the Battle of Punitz (1), resigned all pretensions to the Crown in favour of Stanislas.

Peter, not idle, overruns Poland under Menzikoff. Charles, beaten by the Russians at Pultowa (2), retires to Turkey. Augustus again resumes the Polish Crown. Charles incites the Turks against the Russians, who invest Peter on the banks of the Pruth (3), which compels the Czar to capitulate in 1711. Peter, out of danger, breaks the Treaty, and his Oath, with the Poles by *increasing* his army in Poland.

Augustus, not feeling secure on his throne, applies to Peter to settle the disputes between him and his outraged subjects; when under the dark cloud of Russian terrorism! peace (*misnamed*) was obtained, in 1717, between Augustus on the one side and the Poles on the other. It was then, under a Russian pretext, that Poland's valiant sons were disbanded to the number of 18,000.

Peter by this time had the whole of Livonia in his grasp. A Secret Treaty was formed by Peter and Charles to make a descent upon England, and to add the further acquired appellation of "ARBITER OF EUROPE" to his long list of profaned titles! The death of Charles however, in 1718, put an end to this dangerous Treaty.

Before that Russian Tyrant breathed his last in 1725, he took care to look beyond his grave, fighting even in death to torture poor humanity, and cast his pestilential venom on posterity, by ever propagating endless strife and stratagem within the breasts of his Successors against the liberties of mankind. The WILL! of Peter is that black envenomed scroll that speaks the *Will* of Russia *now* as well as *then!* Was it not *that Will!* looked up to by his successors with a reverential zeal, that struck down POLISH LIBERTY, and dragged her into bondage? Is not *that Will!* the source of Tartar and Hungarian Slavery? And may not *that Will!* ere long prevail against the *Western Sons* of *Liberty*, to Crown a

---

(1) Punitz (Pol. Powiec), a Town of Prussian Poland, 44 m. S. Posen.
(2) Pultowa, Poltava, or Pultawa, a gov. of S. Russia, between lat. 48° 25′ and 51° 6′ N., and lon. 30° 45′ and 36° 40′ E. Poltava, the Cap. on the Vorskla, 70 m. W.S.W. Kharkov.
(3) Pruth, a River of E. Europe, rises in the Carpathian mountains; flows at first E., through Galicia and the Bukovina, and afterwards S.S.E. below Moldavia and Bessarabia, and at Reni, 75 m. from the Black Sea, joins the Danube on the left. Total course, 360 m.

Tyrant Czar the Sovereign of the WORLD! unless the valiant Sons of Freedom break the yoke that hangs around their Polish and Hungarian Brothers? (1)

---

(1) **The WILL of the CZAR (styled) " PETER the GREAT."**

" In the name of the Holy Indivisible Trinity, WE Peter, to all our' successors greeting, &c.: The great God, who always enlightened us by His Divine Wisdom, allows me now to behold *in the Russian nation the people chosen by Providence to govern the whole of Europe!* Most of the European nations have already arrived at a state of extreme *old age*, and they must needs be *regenerated!* by a new and youthful people, *when the time* for the *latter* shall have come," &c. &c.

The following are the RULES! he lays down by which his successors are to follow out the *blood-stained track!* which he himself commenced:—

" **Rule I.**—The Russian Nation is *constantly to be kept* in a state of WAR! and the *warlike spirit* of the Russian Nation to be *kept up!*

" **Rule II.** — *Distinguished* Generals belonging to the most civilised nations of Europe *are to be called* to Russia in time of *War!* and the very first artizans and men of letters in time of peace.

" **Rule III.** — Russia is on all possible occasions to *intermeddle* in EUROPEAN DIFFERENCES, and affairs of *all kinds!* in particular, however, she is to do so in those which concern Germany, on account of the proximity and more direct interest which is to be attached to that country.

" **Rule IV.**— **Poland is to be Divided!** This object in view will be effected by encouraging in that country **Party Rivalries,** and by constantly keeping up a state of **Internal Discord.**

" The most *influential* of the Polish nobility are to be won over with **Gold!** the *influence* in the country, and at the *elections* of the Kings, is to be maintained; and every *opportunity is to be eagerly laid hold of* which affords *a pretext to march Russian* troops into the KINGDOM OF POLAND!

" In the event of the *neighbouring Powers* raising difficulties, the Country should be DIVIDED! and whatever share of the *Spoil!* it may be found necessary *then* to grant to them may always be *resumed hereafter, whenever a proper opportunity offers for the purpose!*

" **Rule V.**—It is expedient to take as much territory as possible from SWEDEN! It must be *separated* from DENMARK! and a feeling of *jealousy is constantly to be kept up* between these two countries.

" **Rule VI.**—The Consorts of the Russian Princes are always to be chosen from amongst the *German* Princesses, in order to multiply the *family connections.*

" **Rule VII.**—The alliance with England, for commercial reasons, is to be preferred to all other alliances. England requires our produce for its navy; and it might moreover be made *subservient* to aid in the *development of the maritime strength of Russia.*

" **Rule VIII.**—It is necessary that the RUSSIAN EMPIRE should be *continually extending* towards the *North*, along the BALTIC; and towards the *South*, along the shores of the BLACK SEA!

" **Rule IX.**—It is expedient to draw as near as possible to CONSTANTINOPLE and to the EAST INDIES. Whoever RULES in these *two Countries* is the TRUE SOVEREIGN OF THE WORLD! Wars are in consequence constantly to be waged, or caused to be waged, against TURKEY and PERSIA; great Colonies are to be established along the EUXINE, in order to get in time the WHOLE BLACK SEA into the *Russian Power!* The same policy is to be followed with regard to the SHORES OF THE BALTIC—*two objects* indispensable for the success of the above project.

" **Rule X.**—THE GREEKS, united and schismatical, who are spread over

On the death of Augustus II., in 1733, the ex-King, Stanislas Leszczynski, was re-elected by the Poles. Passing over the brief and unimportant reigns of Catherine I. and the boy Peter II., we come to that of Anne of Ivanounna, who invaded Poland with an army of 60,000 men for the purpose of raising Augustus III. (Elector of Saxony), son of the late King, to the throne. These savage troops met with success; the Poles being *too* enfeebled to offer resistance by reason of the late *reduction* in their army, when the remaining troops barely numbered 15,000 undisciplined men. Stanislas dethroned, and Augustus III. crowned King of Poland, the Russians besieged Dantzig (1) in 1734, which capitulated after an obstinate and heroic resistance on the part of the besieged Poles of more than five months. The Empress Anne succeeded against the Turks and Tartars; but at a great sacrifice. Elizabeth, the successor of Anne, fought against the Swedes, who evacuated Finland (2), and abandoned the siege of Fredrikshamn (3), when a

---

Hungary, Turkey, and Southern Poland, must be gained by favours to be bestowed on them, for it is *expedient to win their sympathies for Russia!* They must look up to us as their *central point* and their *chief* support. A generally preponderating influence is to be created by joining the principle of Autocracy to a sort of SPIRITUAL SUPREMACY *combined* and *united* in the person of the CZAR. The Greeks will then be *friends* of Russia, and *our* enemies will be *theirs.*

" **Rule XI.**—When SWEDEN is *weakened*, PERSIA *vanquished!* POLAND *subjugated*, TURKEY *conquered*, and the EUXINE and the BALTIC guarded by Russian Fleets, then **Secret Proposals** are *first* to be addressed to the FRENCH COURT, and hereafter to the COURT OF VIENNA, offering them to *share* with Russia the **Kingdom of the World!!**

" If one of those two great Powers consents, from vanity or from flattered ambition, to *entertain the proposal*, then it must be made use of to *suppress the other*, and **to annihilate all other Powers!!!**—an undertaking that cannot fail of success; for by **that time** Russia will already be in possession of the *whole* of the EAST, and of the *major* part of EUROPE!

" **Rule XII.**—Should, however, the impossible become true, and both Powers unite in *resisting* the offer thus made, then it is *expedient* to *incite* them to STRIFE with *one another*, and in this manner to *exhaust their strength*. Then **Russian arms will first inundate Germany, then France, and in this way Europe will and must be conquered!**

" (Signed)   **PETER I.**
" Emperor of all the Russias."

(1) Dantzig (Dantzic Gdansk), an important fortified City and Sea Port of W. Prussia, on the Vistula; lat. 54° 21′ 4″ N., lon. 18° 39′ 34″ E.

(2) Finland (Principality of), an administrative division of the Russian Empire, Cap. Helsingfors, between lat. 59° 48′ and 70° 6′ N., and lon. 20° and 32° E.; bounded N. by Lapland, E. by Archangelsk and Olonetz, S. the Gulf of Finland and the gov. of St. Petersburg, W. by the Gulf of Bothnia and Sweden; area, 136,000 sq. m.

(3) Frederikshamn, or Hamnia, a fortified Sea Port Town of Finland, 32 m. W.S.W. Wyborg.

Treaty of Peace was signed, *giving the greater* portion of Finland *to the Empress* and her *successors!*

In 1752, on the eve of the American war between England and France, those powers looked for an alliance in Europe, when the English Minister, that man of intrigue, Sir Hanbury Williams, proposed the *union* of Russia, Saxony, and Poland!!! Count Broglie counterplotted on behalf of France. The English scheme met with the fate it so justly deserved, being an utter failure, from the bold and determined resolution of those brave and patriotic Polish Generals, Count Branicki and Mokranowski, who well knew the fatal consequences that would attend an alliance with Russia.

A Russian army of 100,000 men marched through Poland on behalf of Augustus III. (the intruder), against Frederick of Prussia, who invaded Saxony. Frederick defeated the Russians at Zorndorff (1) in 1758. The Russians, however, are successful at Zullichau (2) and Custrin (3), when they seize upon Berlin (4). The death of " Elizabeth, falsely styled " the merciful !" terminates the war, when Frederick finds in the person of Peter III., the successor of Elizabeth, a friend and ally. Three Resolutions agreed upon by Peter and Frederick were :—1st. Augustus' successor should be a Pole (the view of the Czartoryskis); 2nd. To protect the Dissidents; 3rd. Russia should resume her possession of Courland (5). In 1762, Peter III. was murdered by his *treacherous* wife Catherine, who, previous to his death, had herself crowned under the title of " Catherine II. the Empress of Muscovy or all the Russias." The Russians, numbering 8,000, encamp at Wilna (6) under a pretext. Mokranowski, on behalf of the Poles, applies to Keyserling, the Russian General, for an explanation. The Russian " GOLD" offered on this occasion, in strict obedience with the mandate or WILL! of

---

(1) Zorndorff is a Village of Prussia, prov. of Brandenburg, 5. m. N. Kustrin.
(2) Zullichau, a walled Town of Prussia, prov. Brandenburg, 50 m. E.S.E. Frankfürt.
(3) Custrin or Küstrin, a fortified Town of Prussia, prov. Brandenburg, 17 m. N.E. Frankfürt.
(4) Berlin, the Cap. of Prussia, of the prov. of Brandenburg, on the Spree, 156 m. E.S.E. Hamburg, and 100 m. N. Dresden; lat. 52° 30′ 16″ N., lon. 13° 23′ 58″; 10 m. in circumference; area, 6,800 acres.
    Courland, or Kurland, a gov. of Russia; lat. 56° and 58° N., and lon. 21° and 27° E. ; area, 10,860 sq. m. ; ceded to Russia in 1795.
(6) Wilna or Vilna, a gov. of Russian Poland; lat. 53° 40′ and 56° 20′ N., and lon. 21° 10′ and 27° E.; area, 27,680 sq. m.; capital, Vilna, formerly cap. of Lithuania, 90 m. N.E. Grodno.

Peter I., had no charms for the noble Mokranowski, who spurned the proffered offer (to sell his Country) as a loathsome pestilence! An ally of the Poles appeared in the person of the Cham of the Crimea, whose threats to Keyserling made the latter withdraw his troops from Lithuania (1).

On the 15th of October, 1763, Augustus III. was no more. Religious dissensions now burst forth between the Roman Catholics and a body called the "Dissidents" of the Protestant party. These latter Catherine takes under her protection. Russia has an understanding with France, Austria, and Prussia, on the point of strict neutrality in reference to Poland. On the 7th of May, 1764, Mokranowski and other Polish Patriots at the elective Diet offer a bold resistance to the election of Stanislas Augustus Poniatowski, and apply to Prince Henry of Prussia to become their King. But Catherine, through her agent Prince Repnin, at the head of 60,000 men on the Polish frontiers, caused a *forced* election of Stanislas on the 7th of September, his coronation taking place on the 25th of November, 1764. The claims of the Dissidents rejected by the Diet of 1776, they apply to Catherine by memorial, who informs the Polish Ambassador that they must get redress, adding, "*I forewarn you, if you do not yield to me what I now request, my demands shall be without bounds!*" On the 20th of March, 1767, the Dissidents, protected by the presence of 40,000 Russians, form a Confederation at Thorn (2). On the 5th of October, 1767, the Diet of the Constitutionalists is opened under the eye of Podosk, the agent of the Muscovite Repnin, where he exhibits his treachery and barbarity, which ends in the banishment to Siberia (3) of those noble Polish Patriots—Soltyk, the Bishop of Cracow; Zaluski, Bishop of Kiow, and others! On the 19th of November, 1767, the Dissidents are confirmed in their rights, on which occasion the Ministers of the foreign Protestant Courts of England, Prussia, Denmark, and Sweden are present to

(1) Lithuania, a Country of Europe, forming all the N. and N.E. part of the ancient Kingdom of Poland, now comprised in the Russian govs. Vitebsk, Moghilev, Vilna, Grodno, and Minsk.

(2) Thorn, a fortified Town of West Prussia, on the River Vistula, 52 m. S.S.W. Marienwerder.

(3) Siberia, Sibiri, or Asiatic Russia, comprises all the N. part of Asia, extending from the Ural Mountains to the Pacific Ocean and Behring Strait, and having S. the Chinese Empire and independent Turkestan, and N. the Arctic Ocean, comprising the islands of New Siberia. Area, 5,393,250 sq. m. Siberia is mostly flat and barren. Winter excessively cold, from 20° to 72° below zero of Fahrenheit.

add importance to the proceedings. On the 29th of February, 1768, the Patriots, in self-defence, formed themselves into that ever-memorable Confederation of Bar (1). Encouraged by France and Austria, they seize Cracow, &c. They send deputies to Saxony, Turkey, and Tartary. They are premature in the publication of their designs, as the Russian troops are everywhere, and intercept their communications. Various engagements take place with the Russians, but victory was always on the side of the Patriots headed by their brave Generals Pulawski and Mokranowski. Catherine denounces the Confederates as "rebels!" and marches a large army against Bar. Pulawski unfortunately was absent from Bar, endeavouring to rally Polocki's routed army, when the Russians attacked the town, which fell in a few days by assault, when 1,200 prisoners were manacled like slaves and sent to Siberia! New Confederations start up in Lithuania, at Lockroczium near Warsaw, and at Cracow. Now a rupture between Russia and Turkey, when the former takes Balta (2) on the frontiers of Podolia, causing great slaughter to the latter. The Turks and Tartars enter the Province of New Servia (3), which the Russians had seized, and carry off 35,000 prisoners. On the 14th of July, 1769, the Russians enter Moldavia (4), rout the Turks, and take Chocium. The Russians then fall back on Poland, where they attack the Confederates, but without success. However, the misfortune of the Turks was a sad blow to the success of the Confederates. For greater security, the Confederates, from their retreat at Bilitz, remove their Council to Eperies (5), in Hungary (6), where they have a fruitless interview with Joseph II. of Austria (7).

(1) Bar, now a Town of Russia, Podolia, 60 m. N.E. Kamenietz.
(2) Balta, now a Town of Russia, in Podolia, on the Kodema, 132 m. E.S.E. Kamenietz.
(3) Servia (Masia Superior, with part of Illyricum), a State of South Europe, cap. Belgrade, nominally included in the Turkish dominions, between lat. 42° 50′ and 45° N., lon. 19° 10′ and 22° 45′ E.; having N. the Danube separating it fiom Hungary, E. Wallachia and Bulgaria, S. Macedonia, and W. Bosnia and Albania.
(4) Moldavia, a Province of European Turkey, in the N.E.: bounded E. and N. by the Pruth, which separates it from Russia; S. by Wallachia and the Danube, which separates it from Bulgaria; and W. by the Austrian Empire.
(5) Eperies (Hung. Herperjes), a royal free Town of Hungary, on the River Tarcza, 143 m. N.E. Pesth.
(6) Hungary (Magyar, Orszag; German, Ungarin; French, Hongrie; ancient Pannonia, &c.), a Country of Central Europe, situated between lat. 44° 43′ and 49° 34′ N., and lon. 14° 25′ and 25° E., cap. Pesth.
(7) Austria, a State of Central Europe, cap. Wien (Vienna), lat. 45° and 51° 2′ N., lon. 8° 35′ and 26° 35′ E.

The Russian campaign of 1770 against Turkey was one on an extensive scale. In February of this year we find the Russian fleet
under Admiral Spiritoff on the coasts of the Peloponnesus (1) ; and
in May, another squadron under Admirals Elphinstone and Dugdale, the former a Scotch, the latter an Englishman. Elphinstone
staked his head to Catherine that he would force the Dardanelles! (2)
On the 5th July, 1770, the Messrs. Elphinstone and Dugdale burn
twenty-five ships of the Turkish fleet in the Straits of Scio; the
latter exposing himself to the flames in a fire-ship during this
villanous undertaking! In June of the same year we find the land
forces of Russia in motion; in *one* place they move from New
Servia and invest Bender, on the Dneister (3) ; in *another* place they
enter Moldavia, and meet with the Turks on the banks of the
Danube. The Turks are defeated for want of skilful Generals.
On the 26th September, 1770, Bender (4) is taken by assault, when
the Confederates again see their hopes blighted. An alliance between
Prussia and Austria, in the persons of Frederic and Joseph, is now
nearly matured from conciliatory interviews they had at Neiss on
the 25th August, 1769, and at Neustadt on the 3rd September,
1770. This alliance was adverse to the cause of the Confederates.
France, under the Duke de Choiseul, was their only ally. In
August 1770, Pulawski, from the Carpathian mountains, makes a
descent on Czenstokow, a fortified abbey on the banks of the
Warta (5). In January 1771, the Russians lay siege to it in a body
4,000 strong, but finally are obliged to raise the siege, leaving 1,200
of their dead behind them. The Confederates now become formidable, occupying several posts of importance. In April 1771, the
Russian campaign against the Turks recommences; but under the
mediation of Austria and Prussia, proposals of peace are made on
the 30th of May, when, by the Treaty of Foktchany, hostilities are

(1) Peloponnesus, or the Morea, Greece or Hellas, ancient Grecia, a Country
of S. Europe, between lat. 36° 23′ and 39° 30′ N., and lon. 20° 45′ and 26° E.
(2) Dardanelles, or Hellespont (Channel of), a narrow Strait between Europe
and Asiatic Turkey, connecting the Sea of Marmora and the Ægean Sea,
between lat. 40° and 40° 30′ N., and lon. 26° 10′ and 26° 40′ E. ; length, 40 m. ;
breadth, 1 to 4 m.
(3) Dniester, Tyras or Danaster, a navigable River of Austria and Russia,
rises in the Carpathian mountains; length, 400 m.
(4) Bender, a fortified Town of Russia, prov. Bessarabia, on the Dneister,
48 m. from its mouth, and 58 m. W.N.W. Odessa.
(5) Warta, or Wartha, a River of Poland and Germany, rises 36 m. N.W.
Cracow.

suspended. In the commencement of this year the Isthmus of Perekop (1) is taken by the Russians under Prince Dalgorucki. A plague brought from Bender by the Russians rages through various parts of the empire, carrying off from 600,000 to 700,000 people. The plague extending to Poland serves as an excuse to Catherine to send further troops there for "*sanitory*" measures. Saladern, the Russian Ambassador at Warsaw, inflicts great cruelties on the Confederates, and designates them "Brigands and Rascals." Towards the close of the year 1771, Viomenil, writing on behalf of the Confederates, states that "All hope depends on the continuation of the War between the Turks and Russians." The Austrians seize Zips (2). The Prussians enter Silesia, and advance on Posen (3) and Thorn. The Confederacy now declines, by reason of the treachery of General Zaremba, who refuses to obey the orders of the Council of the 18th of March, 1772, directing him to attack the Russians at Peterkow, where their troops are disbanded. Prince Jablonowski, their deputy at Vienna, shortly after informs the Confederates, that an alliance was signed between Austria, Russia, and Prussia, for the purpose of partitioning Poland. On the 22nd of April, 1772, the Castle of Cracow had to surrender, when at the same time 10,000 Austrians enter Poland from Hungary, under Count Esterhazy. The famous Confederation of Bar is at length broken up, not so much from the opposition from without as from the *base treachery within!*

Catherine was long the real mistress of Poland; but, out of policy, and apprehending the union of Austria and Prussia against her, and consulting the *Will* of Peter the "Great," she thought it wiser to keep them on her side by making them partakers of the meditated plunder of Poland! The Empress Catherine, when her troops entered Poland in 1767, most solemnly declared that she would maintain the integrity of the Kingdom; and stated, in accordance with the 9th section of the Code, "that *no part* was ever to be *dismembered!*" Catherine *breaks her Oath!* and commissions Frederick to be her agent at Vienna to complete the Triumvirate of Spoliators! Frederick, in the meantime, casts his eyes on the City

(1) Perekop (the Isthmus) connects the Crimea with the mainland of S. Russia, is 20 m. long, and 15 m. across.
(2) Zips, a Village of Hungary, near Kirchdorf.
(3) Posen, a fortified City of Prussia, cap. Grand Duchy Posen, on the Warta and Lowna Rivers, 100 m. E. Frankfurt-on-the-Oder.

of Dantzig; but his contemplations are interrupted by the formidable Treaties signed by Russia, Great Britain, Denmark, and Sweden,
with Dantzig, in 1655, 1707, and 1767, which promised to protect
the commerce of this city. Frederick withdraws in his demands
until a more favourable opportunity presents itself.

On the 17th of February, 1772, the *first* secret Contract of
PARTITION was signed at St. Petersburg between Catherine and
Frederick. On the 4th of March, 1772, the *second* secret Contract
of PARTITION was signed between Prussia and Austria. And on the
5th of August, 1772, the *third* Contract or definite **Treaty of
Partition** was concluded, which regulated the different portions
the Triumvirate were to receive, and which **First Partition**
included *one-third* of the territory of Poland. Russia was to have
the Palatinates of Polock, Witebsk, and Miscislaw to the Dwina
and Dneiper, more than 3,000 square leagues, containing 1,800,000
souls. Austria was to have Gallicia, part of Podolio, and Little
Poland to the Vistula, 2,500 square leagues, containing 2,000,000
souls. Prussia, until she could obtain Dantzig and Thorn, was to
rest satisfied with Polish Prussia and part of Great Poland to the
River Netze, comprising 900 square leagues, containing 860,000
souls. The King Stanislas was to possess the remainder of the
Kingdom of Poland under the old Constitution. In order to shield
their crimes under the sable garb of assumed right or privilege from
the rest of Europe, the three Powers put forward certain " DE-
FENCES." On the 19th of April, 1773, the respective Ministers of this
Triumvirate,—Rewiski, Benoit, Stakelberg,—take upon themselves
to open a Diet of Partition at Warsaw, in the vain hope of obtaining
the sanction of the Polish Nation to this foul act of common
robbery. Although the Russian swords were upraised in the Diet to
govern the debates, the brave Patriots Reyton, Korsack, and others
made themselves heard, when the Diet had to be adjourned until the
17th of May, 1773, and when, against the stifled though antagonistic
voice of the Patriots, Commissioners are appointed to regulate
the Partition of Poland! The Triumvirate Spoliators appoint a
Permanent Council, which ratifies the Treaty of Partition in the
following year. The inactivity of France and England at this
period is remarkable. The dotage of Lewis XV. and weakness of
his Minister answered as the excuse for the *one;* while on the
other hand the English Ministry of the day were deaf to the calls,

entreaties, and solemn warnings poured forth from a body of Patriots
then assembled in London on behalf of oppressed Poland.

In 1778, Catherine, *regardless* of the *Treaty* of Foksani, renews
hostilities against the Turks on the Danube (1). Repulsed under
the walls of Silistria (2), the Russians, reinforced, cross the river.
The Muscovites, under General Roumianstoff, are successful in
many engagements against the Turks, when, by the peace of
Kainardgi, the Black Sea (3) and the Ports of the Turkish Empire
are opened to Russia. The Crimea is now under Muscovite sway.
Troubles again arise in that country between two rival Khans.
Catherine, availing herself of this opportunity, sends fresh troops into
the Crimea, declaring that henceforward that country was under the
"*protection*" of Russia! Catherine now looks northward, and exerts
her influence with Denmark against Sweden. The Turks break the
Treaty of Kaidnargi, when Catherine, out of policy, signs the Treaty
of Constantinople (4), guaranteeing the independence of the Crimea,
and foregoing her intentions on Moldavia and Wallachia. There is
now a war with Austria and Prussia in reference to Bavaria, which
terminates by Catherine espousing the cause of Prussia, when the
Treaty of Tescheu follows. Catherine, and Joseph of Austria, now
form a secret treaty for the invasion of the Crimea. Catherine
builds several towns (Cherson (5), in 1778, among the number) on
the road leading to Constantinople. Catherine breaks the Treaty
of Constantinople, and invades the Crimea under Potampkin, where
she causes the *Butchery* of 30,000 Tartars, regardless of age or sex.
The Crimea, Isle of Tamon, and the Kouban, are in the hands of
Russia. Catherine, having so far acted under the Will of Peter the
"Great" in carrying out his views, raises a monument to her
cherished Predecessor. From the monument of Peter she casts her

(1) Danube (German, Danau; ancient name, Danubius and Ister), next to
the Volga, the largest River in Europe, rises in the Berge, a mountain torrent
in Baden. After a course of 1000 m. it empties itself in the Black Sea.
Navigable for vessels registering 100 tons from Ulm.
(2) Silistria (Turk. Dristra), a City of European Turkey, on the Danube,
57 m. N.E. Schumla.
(3) Black or Euxine Sea, Pontus Euxinus, a great Inland Sea, between
Europe and Asia, within the parallels of lat. 40° 45' and 46° 45' N., lon. 27° 30'
to 41° 50' E.; length, 700 m.; breadth, 380 m.
(4) Constantinople, Stamboul, the Capital of the Turkish Empire, on the
E. extremity of European Turkey, separated by the Bosphorus from Asia
Minor; lat. 41° 16" N., lon. 28° 59' 14" E.; population, 400,000.
(5) Cherson or Kherson, a fortified Town of S. Russia, on the Dneiper, 92 m.
E.N.E. Odessa.

eyes on Persia and China; but her plans are unsuccessful. After her conquests, and to satiate her desires, Catherine visits the Crimea. England and Prussia induce the Turks to take up arms for Catherine's *breach* of the Treaty of Constantinople. The Turks declare War. The Russians capture Oczakow (1), in 1778, after a ten months' siege. Suwarrow, the Russian General, successful at Kisburn, takes Kotchin, on the Dneipor. The Austrians, as the ally of Russia, take Doubitza and Sobach. The Russians, under Admiral Ouchakoff, destroy the Turkish Fleet in the Black Sea to the number of sixty vessels—the crews butchered in a savage manner by Suwarrow. In the meantime, Gustavus, King of Sweden, forms in league with England to surprise St. Petersburg while the war is raging in southern Russia, but is defeated. The King of Denmark, an ally of Catherine, makes war on Sweden, and takes Göttenburg. The Russians seize Bender. The Turks seek peace at Focksani, which is opposed by England and Prussia, who also urge on the Hungarians against Austria. Suwarrow attacks Ismail (2) in 1790, and, after being repulsed on two separate occasions with much vigour by the Turks, he comes again to the assault ; and after sacrificing 15,000 men, who are stretched dead before the place, succeeds in taking Ismail. Suwarrow butchers in cold blood 35,000 Turks, of all ages, male and female, the peaceful inhabitants of Ismail!! The Turks beaten at Motzium, peace is concluded with Russia.

From these barbarous conquests we turn our eyes, with sad anticipations, towards unhappy Poland! In the Diet of 1776, Stanislas, anxious to revise the Constitution, proposes a reform, entrusting the Patriotic Zamoyski with the task. The new Code of laws completed, Zamoyski lays them before the Diet of 1780. The abolition of *monarchial election*, and the *liberum veto* of 1652, which gave the deputies the privilege to suspend all proceedings in the Diet by a simple dissent, formed a prominent feature in the wise Councils of this noble Patriot. The majority of the Polish nobles dissent, who designate Zamoyski a "Traitor!" In May 1787, Stanislas receives an assurance from Catherine and the Emperor of Austria that they would not make the proposed changes in the

---

(1) Oczakow, Otshakov, or Oczakow (Lat. Axiaca), now a Sea-Port Town of S. Russia, on the Black Sea, at the mouth of the Dneiper, 40 m. E.N.E. Odessa.

(2) Ismail, now a Town of Russia, in Bessarabia, on the Kilia or N. arm of the Danube, 40 m. E. Galatz.

Constitution the excuse for another invasion. In August 1787, Catherine, at war with Turkey, suggests an offensive and defensive alliance with Poland, which is referred to the Diet. Frederick William, successor to Frederick the Great, plots with England, Holland, and Sweden, against Russia and Austria. Frederick *pretends* to the Poles that he is in favour of the change in the Constitution, for the purpose of detaching them from Russia. On the 30th of September, 1788, the Constitutional Diet is convoked and confederated. On the 12th of October, the Prussian Minister protests against the Polish league with Russia against Turkey, and offers the alliance of Prussia in its room. The Diet replies that they had no intention of entering into any such alliance with Russia. The Diet, proceeding in their work of reform, Decree an increase to the Army of 100,000 men, demanding at the same time that all Russian troops should quit the Kingdom. The Russian Minister protests, adding, that he "must regard the least change in the Constitution" (*Partition* Constitution!) "of 1775 as a violation of the Treaties." The Prussian Minister, on the other hand, assures the Patriots of Frederick William's *good intentions!* On the 15th of March, 1790, an alliance with Prussia is Decreed by the Constitutional Diet. Frederick William insists that Thorn and Dantzig must be the price of a Commercial Treaty with the Patriots. The Diet, in January 1791, Decree that "no portion of the States of the Republic was ever to be alienated." In April 1791, the towns are admitted by the Diet to the elective franchise, &c.

The 3rd of May, 1791, was that ever-memorable and glorious day when the NEW CONSTITUTION rose into life. Europe awoke from its apathetic trance, and hailed the Era of bright Freedom's Birth! "It is a work," said Fox, "in which every friend to reasonable liberty must be sincerely interested." "Humanity," exclaimed Burke, "must rejoice and glory when it considers the change in Poland!" On the 23rd of May, Frederick William writes to Stanislas an hypocritical approval of the change. The reform, however, so gloriously begun by Stanislas, is exposed to danger by the shaken resolution of that Monarch, which now gives place to low and servile fears! On the 27th of July, 1790, a Treaty of Peace was signed at Reichenbach. This Treaty had a most important influence on European politics. Poland, the centre of the Triumvirate intrigues, by sad experience feels their sting. On the

14th of August, 1790, Russia concludes a peace with Sweden. On the 14th of August Catherine makes peace with the Porte at Jassy (1). The French Revolution breaking out at this time decides the fate of Poland by drawing the Triumvirate bond in closer union. Frederick William, the nominal ally of the Poles, now shows the cloven foot of Treachery ! Catherine, chief of the Triumvirate, makes private and separate arrangements with her co-partners as to not opposing her designs on Poland.   In April 1792, the Deputation for the management of foreign affairs laid an official notice before the Diet, having reference to the hostile preparations of Russia. The Diet, not to be intimidated, continues to reform ; but there are those among the recusant nobles opposed to reform, and who, on the 14th of May, 1792, sign an Act of Confederacy at TARGOWICA in the Russian interest. On the 31st of May, Frederick William writes a letter to Stanislas, in which is portrayed the Prussian Monarch's real character of duplicity. On the 18th of May, 80,000 Russian troops of the line and 20,000 Cossacks are ordered into Poland. The Polish Army was in three divisions :—one under Joseph Poniatoroski, the King's nephew ; the second under Michael Wielkoski ; and the third under the glorious and immortal Kosciusko. The wavering policy of Stanislas now manifests itself, when at a council of war he orders Joseph Poniatowski to retire towards the River Bug (2), in order to concentrate the forces about Warsaw. Several battles with the Russians take place, in which the Poles under Kosciusko had always the advantage. On the 18th of June, 1792, Kosciusko won a brilliant victory at Zielence ; and Mokranowski distinguished himself at the head of the cavalry at Poltuna. At the battle of Dubienka, the most decisive engagement, led on by Kosciusko, the Patriots repelled the enemy, although three times their number. The bravery and prudence of Kosciusko on this day earned for him the admiration of his countrymen. The timid Stanislas gave similar orders of concentration to the army in Lithuania, whereby the Russians advanced unopposed. On the 23rd of July, 1792, the irresolute Stanislas joins the traitorous and more than semi-Russian Confederacy of Targowica, and signs the

---

(1) Jassy, or Yassy, cap. Town of Moldavia, on the Pruth, 200 m. N.N.E. Bucharest.
(2) Bug (or Bog), two Rivers of Russian Poland ; rises in Galicia ; joins the Vistula 18 m. N.W. Warsaw, after a course of 300 m.

Act of the Confederacy, placing Poland once more in the hands of the Russians. The Patriot officers are discharged, the army disbanded, and the people compelled to acknowledge the Confederation and declare against the Constitutional Diet as Despotic. Early in 1793 the Prussians enter Poland, when the Confederates look to Russia to interpose. On the 3rd of February, 1793, some of the Confederates who were not of the sycophants of Catherine repent their rashness, when they issue a protestation against the Prussian invasion. On the 25th of March, 1793, Frederick William issues a manifesto, intimating his intention of seizing Great Poland.

Sievers, the Russian Minister, by the orders of Catherine, connives with the Prussian Minister Bucholz as to a further PARTITION or DISMEMBERMENT of Poland! and on the 9th of April, 1793, those Ministers present to the Commissioners of the Confederates of Targowica, sitting at Grodno, a declaration involving the destiny of Poland. Sievers and Bucholz stated that they had the consent of Austria to *limit* the extent of Poland, and call upon the Poles to accede to this arrangement. The opposition of the Confederates is overcome. The Russian and Prussian Ministers force the Confederates to re-establish the Permanent Council of 1775, which was repealed by the reformers. On the 11th of May, 1793, Sievers and Bucholz compel the Confederacy to pass a Preliminary Law, called *Sancitum*, in order to insure for the Triumvirate Spoliators a *tyrant* majority. It enacted, *first,* that those should *not* be eligible who had not joined the Confederacy; *secondly,* those who had joined the Patriotic or New Constitution were *not* to be admitted. Another Sancitum still harsher passed. To carry out these Laws Russian Troops were ready at a moment's notice. Sievers calls upon the Confederates to sign the Treaty of Partition by the 17th of July. The motion was carried by a tyrant majority of 73 to 20. On the 23rd of July, 1793, the barbarous Treaty, as a matter of course, was signed. The tyranny of Sievers now manifests itself with redoubled cruelty, when the TREATY OF PARTITION is further ratified on the 5th of September, 1793. The majority of the Confederacy, under Muscovite influence, confiscates, plunders, and tyrannises; surpassing even Russia in the enormity of their crimes! But they meet with the reward of their accursed labours; having carried out the wishes of the Tyrant Catherine, who, no longer requiring their assistance, throws them off, and directs this traitorous

Confederacy of Targowica to be dissolved! On the 23d of November, 1793, the Concession of the Diet of the glorious Constitution takes place, the Confederacy of Targowica having paved the way for its downfall!

We now come to the **Second Partition or Dismemberment of Poland!** The Triumvirate Spoliators having, as before stated, seized in 1773 of the *then* territory *one-third*, on the Second Partition, towards the close of 1793, two of them seize about *one-half* of the remaining portion ;—Catherine extending her portion of the spoil to Central Lithuania and Volhynia ; Frederick William taking as his share the remainder of Great and a portion of Little Poland. Stanislas had the remnant of his shattered Kingdom *secured* to him under the old laws!

We now find the Polish Patriots as Refugees at Leipzig, of whom the most prominent are—the noble Kosciusko, Dzialinski, Kollontay, Mostowski, Malachowski, and Potocki. They there await, with anxious minds and throbbing hearts, the favoured moment of their Country's Call! Their Brother Patriots in Poland are not long in sending for their aid. A Patriotic Conspiracy is formed at Warsaw. Their plans, assisted by a general agency throughout the Kingdom, are nearly matured ; but Igolstrum, the Russian Minister and successor of Sievers, being invested with absolute power, demands the reduction of the Polish Army of 30,000 men to 15,000. The Permanent or Partition Council of 1775 issues the orders of this Minister, which serve as the signal or give the impetus for Patriotic action.! On the 15th of March, 1794, Madalinski, stationed at Pultusk (1) with 700 cavalry, refuses to disband. He now traverses the Prussian territory, levying contributions and making many prisoners, and proceeds to Cracow. Kosciusko hastens from Saxony; and on the night of the 23rd of March enters Cracow, where Wodzicki, at the head of a body of troops, is stationed to receive him. On the 24th of March, 1794, Kosciusko, by virtue of a Deed of Insurrection, is appointed " DICTATOR AND GENERALISSIMO OF POLAND."

The 12th of February, 1746, was the day that smiled upon the Birth of Thadeus Kosciusko, born of a noble Lithuanian family. As he advanced to early manhood, his heart became enamoured

---

(1) Pultusk, or Pultowsk, a Town of Poland, 60 m. E.N.E. Plock.

with the charms of a lovely maid, the daughter of the Marshal of Lithuania. But the ardent hopes of this noble lover were doomed to disappointment! When in happy converse they would meet, Kosciusko beholding in this Patriotic maid a sentiment so congenial with his own—a love of country!—that the too susceptible heart of the noble Patriot dreamt that he saw another charm concealed within her breast: but, alas! his fond and cherished hopes were blighted! her heart was not attuned to his in this respect; his vision of connubial bliss had vanished; her love was not reciprocal with Kosciusko's, when Prince Lubomirski became the accepted suitor. To banish the grief he felt, and to forget the love he formed, he repairs to France. He returns again to Poland; after which we find him in America, fighting in the ranks of Washington and Gates. Kosciusko, again in Poland, now holds (by the appointment of the Diet) the rank of Major-General in the campaign of 1792.

On the 4th of April, 1794, the memorable battle of Raclawice was fought, which lasted five hours, when 4,000 Poles, with Kosciusko at their head, gained the glorious day. On that occasion 3,000 Russians are killed, and many prisoners captured; eleven cannon together with a standard taken.

Igolstrum directs Stanislas to issue a proclamation denouncing the Patriots. On the 16th of April, 1794, Igolstrum sends a Letter (1) to the Minister of War at St. Petersburg, which portrays the apprehensions of that Minister On the same day Igolstrum directs the Permanent (or Partition) Council of 1775 to cause the arrest of twenty of the most distinguished persons whom he named: at the same time he commands the Grand General to disarm the Polish Garrison at Warsaw. The 18th of April, the Festival of Easter Eve, was the day fixed upon to carry out this treacherous plot, when the inhabitants would be at mass. Kalinski, an inhabitant of Warsaw, fortunately discovers the plan, and informs the Patriots that Russians, in Polish uniforms, were to compose the guards which on such occasions are stationed at the churches. On the 17th of April the Patriots, anticipating the evil intentions of their opponents, cause an Insurrection. At 4 o'clock in the morning a body of Patriots attack the Russian guards and seize the Arsenal and Powder Magazine, and arm the inhabitants. For two

_____

(1) See Act i. Sc. iv. page 23.

days a bloody encounter takes place; and although the Russians are far superior in numbers, being 8,000 strong, the Patriots are victorious, when they expel the remnant of the Muscovites after killing 2,200 and making 2,000 prisoners. On the 23rd of April, 1794, Jasinski attacks the Russians at Wilna, and, after another bloody encounter, the Patriots obtain possession of the place. The Prussians, 40,000 strong, headed by Frederick William, join the Russians near Szczekocing (1).

In ignorance of the junction formed between the Russian troops, Kosciusko marches to the relief of Cracow at the head of 16,000 regulars and 10,000 peasants; the combined forces of the allies outnumbering the Patriots by 30,000 men. On the 6th of June, 1794, the battle of Szczekocing takes place, when, after some hours' cannonade, the Poles make good their retreat with the loss of 1,000 men. On the 9th of June the Patriots suffer at Chelm. On the 15th of June the Russian and Prussian forces take Cracow. On the 27th of June barbarities are enacted at Warsaw by reason of some evil-inclined and seditious persons inciting the minds of the rabble, who break open the jails and massacre a great number of the prisoners. Kosciusko signs the death-warrant ordering the ringleaders to be hung. On the 13th of June the Austrians march an Army into Little Poland. Kosciusko encamps at Wola. The King of Prussia invests Warsaw. The Prussians and Russians, 50,000 strong, encamp near Wola. On the 27th of July, 1794, one of a series of combats takes place,—repeated on the 1st and 3rd of August, when the Prussians attempt to bombard Warsaw. Dombrowski successful in some late skirmishes with the Russians at Czerniakow (2); again attacks them, but is obliged to retire. Many warm encounters take place, when Dombrowski, Prince Joseph, Poniatowski, and several others bravely, distinguish themselves. On the night of the 28th of August the hottest encounter took place, in which Dombrowski was attacked at the same time as Zajonczek was marching against the Prussians, when the heroic valour of the Poles surmounted all obstacles. On the 5th of September, 40,000 Prussians (3) make a sudden retreat towards the

(1) Szczekociny, or Szczuczin, a Town of Poland, 35 m. S.W. Augustowo.
(2) Czerniakow, or Czerniejevo, a Town of Prussia Poland, 10 m. S.W. Gnesen.
(3) See Letter to Kosciusko from Dombrowski, Act iv. Sc. i. p. 67.

Polish Provinces recently annexed to Prussia, in order to put down
an insurrectionary movement that had taken place there. The
Insurgent Chiefs in Great Poland, — Mniewski, Castellan of
Kuinewia, &c.—communicate with their Brother Patriots. For five
months they form magazines of arms and ammunition in some
secluded woods. On the 23rd of August, 1794, a body of these
Patriots assembled in a wood near Sieradz (1), attacked the Prussian
guards, and took the town. On the 25th of August, Mniewski,
with a company of resolute Patriots, march to Wloclawek (2), where
they capture thirteen Prussian barques laden with ammunition for
the siege of Warsaw. The glorious rays of Patriotism rekindle the
ardour of the Dantzites and Brethren of Silesia. Dombrowski sent
by Kosciusko to aid the insurgents, and, after many encounters
with the enemy, succeeds, by the 15th of September, 1794, in
regaining Great Poland.

Alas! the Sun of Freedom has begun to set in Lithuania. On
the 12th of August, Wilna was taken by the Russians with an
overwhelming force! the remainder of the Province shortly after
witnessing the same disasters. Suwarrow, directed by the rapacious
Catherine to annihilate the Revolution, marches from the frontiers
of Turkey towards Warsaw. On the 16th of September, Suwarrow
attacks a body of the Patriots at the village of Krupozyce, and
drives them on to Brzesclitewski. The engagement is renewed on
the following day, when the Patriots are overwhelmed by the compact masses of the enemy. This last defeat opens the road to
Warsaw. Kosciusko advances to the aid of the flying army. When
at Grodno (3), Kosciusko appoints Mokranowski to the command
of the Lithuanian army. Kosciusko hastens to prevent the junction
of Suwarrow and Ferzen.

On the 10th of October, 1794, the Battle of Macieiowice (4), the
last in the brilliant career of Kosciusko, takes place. Though a sad
and fatal day for Poland, still it was a day on which a glorious and
immortal effort was made to stem the rapid torrent of invasion!
The Battle was long, fierce, and bloody! Victory held its doubtful

(1) Sieradz, a Town of Poland, on the Warta, 32 m. E.S.E. Kalice.
(2) Wloclawek, a Town of Poland, on the Vistula, 30 m. N.W. Plock.
(3) Grodno, a Town of Russia, on the right bank of the Niemen, 90 m.
S.S.W. Vilna.
(4) Macieiowice, a Town of Poland, on the Vistula, 45 m. S.W. Siedlec.

c

reign for many an hour. The Traitor Poninski! with the expected
troops had not arrived! Kosciusko finds himself betrayed! A
hurried Council of War assembles, at which Madalinski and
Kosciusko are agreed upon forming a *Forlorn Hope!* when with a
last great effort to turn the adverse front of battle, Kosciusko, joined
by his general officers, dashes onward through the thickest of the
fight ; and after cutting through column after column of the enemies'
ranks, and at length *overwhelmed by increasing numbers and loss of
blood, Kosciusko falls, in defence of his Country, pierced and covered
with wounds !*

On the 4th of November, 1794, after an obstinate and heroic
resistance on behalf of the besieged, when 8,000 Poles perish sword
in hand, Suwarrow takes Praga, and butchers the peaceful inhabitants,—including men, women, and children,—to the number of
12,000! On the 6th of November, Warsaw, weakened, capitulates,
The Prisoners taken by the Russians are confined in the jails of
St. Petersburg, or driven to Siberia. The Prisoners taken by the
Prussians are doomed to pine away in the fortresses of Glogan (1).
And Austria entombs the Patriots in the dungeons of Olmutz! (2)

On the 24th October, 1795, the Treaty for the **Third Partition of Poland** was concluded, but not finally arranged
between Austria and Prussia until the 21st of October, 1796. By
this Partition, Russia seizes the remainder of Lithuania, Samagotia,
and Chelm, to the right of the River Bug, and the rest of Wollhynia.
Austria seizes the Palatinates of Cracow, Sandomir, and Lublin, with
a portion of Chelm and parts of the Palatinates of Masovia, Brzesc,
and Polachia, on the *left* bank of the Bug. Prussia has the parts
of Polachia and Masovia on the *right* bank of the Bug ; part of the
Palatinate of Samogitia and Troki on the Niemen ; and a district of
Little Poland. The Rivers Vistula (3), Niemen (4), Bug, and
Pilica (5), form the lines of demarcation by which we ascertain the
respective possessions of the Triumvirate Spoliators at that period.

---

(1) Glogan, Glogau, or Gross-Glogau, a strongly fortified Town of Prussian
Silesia, 35 m. N.N.W. Leignitz, on the River Oder.
(2) Olmutz (Moravian, Holomauc), a strongly fortified City of Moravia, on
the River March, 40 m. N.E. Brüm.
(3) Vistula (Germ. Weichsel), an European River, rises in the Carpathian
mountains, and after a course of 530 m., traversing Poland and W. Prusaia,
enters the Baltic.
(4) Niemen, or Memel, a River of Russian Poland, rises in Minsk, and,
after a course of 400 m., enters the Baltic 30 m. W. Tilsit.
(5) Pilica, a branch of the Vistula.

On the 28th of November, 1794, Stanislas Augustus Poniatowski, the last of Poland's Kings, is forced by the Russian Ambassador at Grodno to sign a Deed of Abdication, when Catherine grants him a pension of 200,000 ducats.

Catherine now directs her thoughts against Republican France in league with Gustavus III. of Sweden ; but that Monarch's death interrupted her plans of invasion. Catherine joins the English against the French with eight frigates and twelve old ships of the line. She now turns to the East, invading Persia in the Province of Daghestan (1). She next turns her attention to another plan for invading the Turkish Empire. By recent Treaties with Austria and England these Powers engage with Russia to aid her projects against Turkey, on the proviso that Catherine joins them against France.

On the 16th of November, 1796, Catherine, after a struggle with her wicked conscience, when she is supposed to have beheld a vision portraying the pallid and agonised features of her murdered husband, departs this life, with a Tyrant's death-shriek, in an apoplectic fit!

Catherine is succeeded by her son, Paul I. England joins Paul in a coalition against France. The Russian army, 50,000 strong, headed by Suwarrow, marches from Gallicia against the French. The Austro-Russian army obtain a victory against the French at Verona (2). The French, under Moreau, are again beaten at Cassano (3). On the 8th of September, 1798, the Austro-Russian army are defeated at Bassagnano (4). Suwarrow marches on Turin (5). On the 19th of June, 1799, the French, under Macdonald, are defeated at the battle of Trebia (6) by the Austro-Russian army after a sanguinary encounter of two days' duration. The Tuscans and Ligurians join the Austrians and Russians against the French, as also the Piedmontese and Lombards. The French, under the young Joubert, are beaten, but afterwards they commit a frightful havoc of the Russians! No less than four armies proceed from

(1) Daghestan, now a Province of Russia, extends along the W. coast of the Caspian Sea, lat. 41° and 43° N., lon. 46° and 50°.
(2) Verona, a fortified City of Austrian Italy, gov. Venice, on the River Adige, 22 m. N.N.E Mantua.
(3) Cassano comprises several Villages in N. Italy, 23 m. N.W. Milan.
(4) Bassagno, or Bassano, a Town of Italy, 19 m. N.E. of Vicenza.
(5) Turin (Ital. Turina; anc. Augusta, Turinorum), a Town of N. Italy, Piedmont, on the left bank of the River Po, 79 m. W.S.W. of Milan.
(6) Trebia, a large Plain on the banks of a river of the same name, which rises on the N. side of the Apennines, 10 m. N.E. Genoa.

Asia to subjugate France. The Austrians defeat Jourdan at Ostrach. Massena retreats and crosses the Limmat (1). The Austrians seize Zurich (2). On the 26th of August, the ever-memorable battle of Zurich is fought, when the gallant soldiers of the French Republic defeat the Russians and Austrians under their immortal General Massena. The Russians under Suwarrow are defeated at the battle of Dissenhofen, when they are obliged to retreat with the small remnant (12,000) of their large army. The Emperor Paul becomes enraged at the total defeat of his armies by the French. On the 14th of June, 1800, Napoleon defeats the Austrians at the memorable battle of Marengo (3). Paul, after the decisive battle of Marengo, becomes an admirer of Napoleon. A Treaty of armed neutrality is signed between Russia and Sweden. In 1801, the Treaty of Luneville (4) takes place between Napoleon and the Emperor of Austria. It was after this treaty that the English Minister Pitt resigned. Paul I. now prepares on a large scale to attack British India (5) in Asia, and takes the route through Persia for obtaining the object of his ambitious designs, when the assassin's hand puts an end to this daring project. At the hour of half-past eleven o'clock, on the night of the 24th of March, 1801, Paul I., Emperor of all the Russias, was strangled by several conspirators in the Palace of St. Michael, Petersburg.

We will now retrace our steps, and take a glance at Poland after its Fall in 1794. The Patriots who were fortunate enough to escape the Triumvirate Gaolers repaired to Paris and Venice, where the French Directory promise them assistance. On the 5th of April, 1795, a Treaty took place between France and Prussia at Bâle (6) which shook the confidence of the Polish Patriots. They were satisfied, however, when they were informed that there was no mention made of Poland in the Treaty. A Polish Confederacy is formed in Paris under Francis Bares, the Polish agent ; and a corresponding

---

(1) Limmat, a River of Switzerland, Canton of Zurich, rises in Lake Zurich, and continues 18 m., when it joins the Aar, 2 m. E. Brugg.
(2) Zurich, cap. of the Canton of Zurich (anc. Turicum), on the Limmat, 60 m. N.E. Bern.
(3) Marengo, a Village of Piedmont, 2 m. S.E. Alessandria.
(4) Luneville, a Town of France, on the Vezouze, 15 m. S.E. Nancy.
(5) India (British), comprehends, for the most part, the Peninsula deno-minated Hindostan ; the British territory into the Presidencies of Bengal, Madras, and Bombay ; also the Islands of Ceylon, Singapore, and Borneo.
(6) Bâle (Germ. Basle), a City in the N. of Switzerland, on the Rhine, 43 m. N.E. of Bern.

one in Venice, under the protection of the French ambassador. Oginski repairs to Constantinople from Paris, to negotiate with the Ottoman Court on behalf of the Polish Patriots. The plan of the negotiation not meeting with success, the Polish Confederacy in Wallachia is dissolved. The Emperor Paul I., on his accession, liberates the Polish captives. Prussia, since the Treaty of Bâle, liberates her captives. Austria, however, is hardened against this act of clemency. In September 1796, Dombrowski in Paris lays a plan before the Directory for forming the memorable POLISH LEGION, in union with France, against Russia and Austria in Italy. On the 7th of January, 1797, Buonaparte signs an Agreement at Milan (1) with the Provisional Government in reference to taking the Polish Legions into pay, when they are engaged in Lombardy (2) and Rome. On the 18th of April, 1797, a Treaty of Peace is concluded between France and Austria at Leoben (3), which serves as another cause for Polish misgivings. On the 17th of October, 1797, another Treaty was signed, at Camp-Formio (4), between the French and Austrians, which was another sad blow to the Poles. On the 3rd of May, 1799, the *First* Polish Legion enters Rome. On the 28th of July, the *Second* Polish Legion were defeated by the united Austro-Russian forces. On the 15th of August, 1799, the Polish Legion suffered great loss at the battle of Novi (5).

On the 11th of November, 1799, Buonaparte is raised to the Consulship of France. Dombrowski repairs to France, and forms seven new battalions of the Polish Legions. On the 3rd of December, 1800, the memorable battle of Hohenlinden (6) is fought by the French, under Moreau, against the Austrians, when a brilliant victory is obtained by the former, owing, in a great measure, to the gallant fighting of the Polish Legion under General Kniaziewicz.

On the 24th of March, 1801, Alexander I., eldest son of Paul I., ascended the throne of all the Russias. Buonaparte declares war

(1) Milan (Ital. Milano, Germ. Mailand. anc. Mediolanum), a City of Austrian Italy, cap. of the Lombardo Venetian Kingdom, lat. 45° 28′ 1″ N., lon. 9° 11′ 20″ E.
(2) Lombardy forms the W. part of the Lombardo Venetian Kingdom, E. part of Piedmont, and the Duchies of Parma and Modena.
(3) Leoben, a Town of Austria, Styria, 9 m. W.S.W. Brück on the Mur.
(4) Camp-Formio (or Campo-Formio), a Village of N. Italy, 7 m. S.W. Udine.
(5) Novi, forming three towns at the foot of the Apennines, in the plain of Marengo, 14 m. S.E. Alessandria.
(6) Hohenlinden, a Village of Upper Bavaria, 20 m. E. Munich.

against Prussia. On the 14th of October, 1806, the battle of
Jena (1) is fought, when Napoleon's grand army entirely routed
the Prussians, and at which battle the Duke of Brunswick, on the
Prussian side, fell. The French occupy Berlin. The Poles drive
the Prussians from Kalisz and other forts. On the 16th of
November, 1806, Dombrowski forms four regiments at Posen. The
Russian General Benningen is compelled to retreat from Prussian
Poland. On the 28th of November, 1806, the French, under
Murat, enter Warsaw. On the 18th of December, Napoleon enters
Warsaw. He defeats the Russians at Pultusk and Golymin. On
the 14th of June, 1807, Napoleon defeats the Russians and Prussians
at the sanguinary battle of Friedland (2). On the 7th of July,
1807, the remarkable Treaty of Tilsit (3) is concluded between
France, Russia, and Prussia, when a great portion of Prussian
Poland under said Treaty is declared *Independent*, under the
denomination of the Grand Duchy of Warsaw, comprising 1,800
square leagues. Frederick Augustus, the Elector of Saxony, whom
Napoleon made King of Saxony, on the 11th of December, 1806, is
appointed by him the Grand Duke of Warsaw. On the 22nd of
July, 1807, Napoleon approves of the Code regulating the NEW
CONSTITUTION. On the 10th of March, 1809, the first Diet of the
New Constitution is held. On the 6th of April, 1809, Austria
declares war against France. On the 20th of April the Austrians,
30,000 strong, defeat Prince Poniatowski with only 10,000 men at
Raszyn, when they enter Warsaw with the Archdude Ferdinand at
their head. Prince Poniatowski invades Gallicia or Austrian Poland.
On the 14th of May, 1809, he marches into Lublin; and on the
19th of May takes Sandomir by assault. On the 24th of May the
Poles enter Leopol, when they are met by the people as deliverers
with tears of joy. All Gallicia is now up in arms against their
oppressors! On the 14th of May, Dombrowski defeats the
Austrians at Thorn. On the night of the 1st of June the Austrians
retreat. On the 16th of July, a great part of Gallicia is added to
the Grand Duchy of Warsaw. On the 14th of October, another

(1) Jena, a Town of Central Germany, Duchy of Saxe-Weimar, on the
Saale, 12 m. E.S.E. Weimar.
(2) Friedland, a Village of E. Prussia, 27 m. S.E. Königsberg.
(3) Tilsit, a Town of E. Prussia, on the Niemen, or Memel, 60 m. N.E.
Königsberg.

Treaty of Peace was signed at Vienna between Austria and France,
which is the cause of fresh misgivings on the part of the Poles.

On the 14th of March, 1812, a Treaty is signed at Vienna between
Napoleon and the Emperor of Austria, in reference to Gallicia in
Poland. Alexander I. acts with clemency towards the Lithuanians,
and *promises them certain rights and privileges which were never
realised!* On the 26th of June, 1812, Prince Adam Czartoryski is
nominated Marshal by the Diet of Warsaw; and on the same day
Napoleon enters Wilna, on his way to Moscow, when he gives an
evasive reply to the Polish deputation that waited upon him to
ascertain more fully his views in reference to Poland. On the
15th of August, 1812, a Confederacy is formed at Wilna, under
Napoleon's direction, independent of the Duchy of Warsaw. On
the 7th of September, 1812, Napoleon gained a great victory over
the Russians at Borodino (1), which is generally called the battle of
Moskwa. The French then enter Moscow (2), which is set on fire
by direction of the Russian General, when the French are obliged
to make a disastrous retreat. On the 3rd of December, 1812,
Buonaparte deserts his sadly depopulated army, and proceeds to
Warsaw, and from thence to Paris. On the 10th of December,
1812, the Russians enter Wilna and Warsaw. On the 20th of
December, the Diet of Warsaw give the office of Commander-in-
Chief of the Polish army to Prince Joseph Poniatowski. Out of
the 70,000 Poles that joined the French in the invasion of Russia
there is still a remnant of 22,000. On the 7th of February, 1813,
Prince Poniatowski leaves Warsaw with his army, and marches for
Cracow. On the 18th of April, 1813, Buonaparte, in Saxony, is
prepared for battle. On the 10th of June, 1813, Prince Poniatowski's
army joins Buonaparte at Zittau (3). On the 26th and 27th
of August, 1813, Napoleon defeats the Allies under the walls of
Dresden (4). On the 16th and 18th of October, the Allies defeat
the French at the battle of Leipzig (5). Prince Poniatowski, when

(1) Borodino, a Village of Russia, on the River Kologa, 75 m. W.S.W. Moscow.
(2) Moscow (Russ. Moskwa), the ancient Capital of Russia, on the River
Moskwa, 397 m. S.E. St. Petersburg, lat. 55° 45' 13" N., lon. 37° 37' 54" E.
Moscow was founded in the 12th century, and, after it was set on fire in 1812,
has been since rebuilt on a more regular plan.
(3) Zittau, a Town of Saxony, on the River Mandau, 26 m. S.E. Bautzen.
(4) Dresden, the Capital of Saxony, on the Elbe, 61 m. E.S.E. Leipzig, and
100 m. S.S.E. Berlin.
(5) Leipzig, or Leipsic, the second City of Saxony, on the River White
Elster, 18 m. S.E. Halle. Leipsic is the celebrated Germanic book emporium.

retreating with the French, is unfortunately drowned in the River Pleisse (1). On the 30th of October, 1813, the French under Napoleon, in concert with the remnant of the Polish Legion, are victorious at the battle of Hanau (2). The Polish Legions follow Napoleon to France, who, at the Treaty of Fontainebleau (3) in 1814, abdicates. On the 25th of August, 1814, Dombrowski leaves France for Posen. The Emperor Alexander raises his brother, the Grand Duke Constantine, to the rank of Commander-in-Chief of the Polish Legions. On the 3rd of May, 1815, the Congress of Vienna was held, which declared the Duchy of Warsaw should be formed into a Kingdom in union with the Russian Empire, having however a *Separate* Constitution. By said Treaty Eastern Gallicia was ceded to Austria,—the territory of Cracow to have a *Separate* Constitution. Prussia's share was under the Grand Duchy of Posnania. Alexander issues a Proclamation on the 25th of May, and is proclaimed King of Poland at Warsaw on the 20th of June, 1815. Alexander arrives at Warsaw in November 1815; and on the 24th of December the New Constitution is established. However, Lithuania, Posnania, Cracow, and Gallicia, received *no benefit* or participation in this beneficial change in the Duchy of Warsaw, ALTHOUGH THE TREATY OF VIENNA HELD OUT CERTAIN PROMISES WHICH WERE NEVER FULFILLED! On the 15th March, 1818, the first Diet of the Constitution was held. On the 31st of July, 1819, certain innovations take place contrary to the spirit of the New Constitution, when, among other encroachments of Russian authority, the *Suppression of the Press!* is the most formidable. Among other additions to the Russian territory in Asia which take place during Alexander's reign, the most important was that of Georgia (4) in 1802, and Mingrelia (5) and Imiritia (6) in 1804; and in the North of Europe he made

(1) Pleisse, a River of Saxony, forming a junction at Leipzig with the White Elster.
(2) Hanau, a Town of Germany, province of Hessen-Cassel, on the Kinzig, 86 m. S.S.W. Cassel.
(3) Fontainebleau, a Town of France, surrounded by a magnificent forest, 35 m. S.S.E. Paris
(4) Georgia, or Grusia. a Country belonging to Russia, in the Caucasus, W. Asia, comprising the Western and Central portion of Transcaucasia, between lat. 40° and 42° 30′ N., and lon. 43° and 47° E.; area, 21,500 sq. m.
(5) Mingrelia, a Province of Asiatic Russia, bounded on the N. by the Caucasus, on the E. by Imertia, on the S. by Guiræ, and on the W. by the Euxine.
(6) Imiritia, a Province of Asiatic Russia, Transcaucasia, bounded on the N. by the Caucasus mountains, on the E. by Georgia, on the W. by Mingrelia and Guriel, and on the S. by Akalzikh.

further aggressions in Finland in 1808. On the 1st of December, 1825, Alexander I. departs this life. After an interregnum of some months, Nicholas, the brother of Alexander, on the 8rd of December, 1826, is crowned Emperor and Autocrat of all the Russias. Nicholas now commences an Asiatic war, and under General Madatoff routes the Persians on the Banks of the River Shamkora, when Elizabetopol (1) is retaken by the Russians; the Persians retreating over the Araxes (2). Hostilities recommenced in the beginning of 1827, when Erivan (3) was taken by the Russians under Prince Paskiewitch. On the 20th of October, 1827, the combined fleets of Russia, France, and England obtained a victory over the Turkish and Egyptian fleets at the battle of Navarino (4). Prince Paskiewitch marches to Teheran (5), when a Treaty of Peace is entered into with Persia, at Turcomanchai, in February 1828. By this Treaty it was agreed that the River Aras should be the line of demarcation between the territories of Russia and Persia. The important territories of Nukhchivan and Erivan, which were taken by the Russians in 1827, were confirmed to them by said Treaty, as also the Provinces of Moghan and Talish (6), &c. Persia, by this Treaty, had to give up her navy in the Caspian Sea, besides paying the whole expenses of the war.

On the 4th of April, 1828, Russia declares war against Turkey, on the ground, as stated in the manifesto issued by Nicholas, of the Turkish violation of the Treaty of Akerman (7), which was entered into in April 1826. Said manifesto also asserts further infractions of the Ottomans, in reference to the Treaties of the 28th of May, 1812, and 1783,—one of peace, and the other of commerce,—and other excuses to justify the AGGRESSIVE character of Russia. The Russian invasion of Wallachia and Moldavia takes place. The

---

(1) Elizabetopol, or Ganjeh, a fortified Town of Georgia, 90 m. S.E. Teflis.
(2) Araxes, or Aras, a River of Armenia, rises in Erzeroum, near lat. 40° 30′ N., and lon. 41° 10′ E., divides the territories of Russia and Persia, and, after a rapid course of 500 m.. flows into the Caspian Sea.
(3) Erivan, a fortified Town of Russian Armenia, on the Zengui, 115 m. S.S.W. Teflis.
(4) Navarino, or Navarin, a fortified Sea Port Town of Greece, Morea, gov. Pylos, on a Mediterranean bay, 6 m. N. Modon.
(5) Teheran, or Tehran, the Capital of Persia, 70 m. S. of the Caspian Sea, and 210 m. N. of Ispakan, lat. 35° 42′ N., lon. 51° 20′ 50″ E.
(6) Talish, an Asiatic Province of Russia, lat 38° and 39° N., and lon. 48° and 49° E.
(7) Akerman, Tyras, a fortified Town of Russia, in the Province of Bessarabia, on the Dniester, 20 m. S.W. Odessa, lat. 46° 11′ 51″ N., lon. 30° 21′ 52″ E.

Danube and Pruth are crossed; Bucharest (1) and Jassy captured; Brahilov (2), after a valiant resistance on behalf of the Turks, was captured by the Russians in the month of June 1828; and Shumla (3) was invested, but without success. Varna (4) was taken in October 1828, after a siege of three months. The Russians, in Asia, capture Akhalkalaki (5), Kars (6), and the city of Akhalzikh (7), &c. In the month of May 1829, Silistria (8) is taken by the Russians, who fortify it. The battle of Kulevitch takes place, and, after lasting nearly two days, the Russians defeat the Turks. The Russians cross the Balken (9). The Russians in Asia take Erzeroum (10), which capitulates on the 27th of June, 1829. The Turks by this war lost 130,000 men,—the Russians 80,000. On the 24th of May, 1829, Nicholas is crowned King of Poland at Warsaw. On the 20th of August, 1829, Enos (11) is taken by the Russians. On the 14th of September, 1829, the Treaty of Andrinople (12) is concluded, by which Nicholas had secured to him Anapa (13) and Poti (14), with a considerable extent of coast on the Euxine. About this time there was a secret understanding between the French Monarch and Nicholas to aid the latter in his designs against Turkey by seizing Constantinople. On the 27th of July, 1830, the Revolution breaks out in Paris, when Charles X. is

(1) Bucharest, Bukharest, or Bukhorest, a City of S.E. Europe, cap. of Wallachia, lat. 44° 25′ 39″, lon. 26° 5′ 24″ E.

(2) Brahilov, or Brailoff (Turk. Ibrahil), a Town and Port of Wallachia, on the Danube, 130 m. N.E. Bucharest.

(3) Shumla (Marcianopolis), a fortified City of European Turkey, 58 m. S.S.W. Silistria.

(4) Varna (Odessus), a fortified Sea Port Town of European Turkey, Bulgaria, on the Euxine, lat. 43° 12′ 2″ N., lon. 27° 56′ 2″ E., 47 m. E. of Shumla.

(5) Akhalkalaki, a Town and Fort of Russian Armenia, 30 m S.E. Akhalzikin.

(6) Kars, a City of Asiatic Turkey, 105 m. N E. Erzeroum.

(7) Akhalzikh, a City of Asiatic Russia, in the Province of Georgia, lat. 41° 40′ N., lon. 43° 1′ E., 103 m. W. Tiflis.

(8) Silistria (Turk. Dristra), a City of European Turkey in Bulgaria, on the Danube, 57 m. N.N.E. of Shumla.

(9) Balken, or Balkan (Hæmus), an extensive mountain chain of European Turkey, extending from the town of Sophia in Bulgaria, lon. 23° E., to Cape Emineh on the Euxine.

(10) Erzeroum, a Subdivision of Asiatic Turkey, between lat. 39° and 41°, and lon. 39° and 44° E.

(11) Enos (or Eônos, Ænos), a Sea Port Town of Turkey in Europe, 38 m. N.W. Gallipoli, on the Ægean Sea.

(12) Adrinople (Hadrianopolis), a City of Turkey in Europe, on the Tundja, lat. 41° 41′ 26″ N., lon. 26° 35′ 41″, 137 m. N.W. Constantinople.

(13) Anapa, a Sea Port Town and Fortress of Circassia, on the Euxine, lat. 44° 54′ 52″ N., lon. 37° 16′ 21″ E., 47 m. S.E. Venikale.

(14) Poti, a Fort of Asiatic Russia, gov. Transcaucasia, on the River Rion, near the Euxine.

obliged .to abdicate, and goes into exile. The barbarities of the
Grand Duke Constantine, the brother of Nicholas and viceroy of
Poland,—together with the many infringements that take place in
the New Constitution,—arouse the indignant spirit of the Poles,
when a Revolution, encouraged by the Parisian Revolution, breaks
out in Warsaw on the 29th of November, 1830. The first move
was the attack made on Constantine's Palace by eighteen students,
who were unsuccessful in their attempt to seize Constantine : however, they attack the barracks in company with the engineers, and,
after a bloody encounter, are victorious. A national Government
is formed, at the head of which Prince Adam Czartoryski is nominated President. On the 5th of December, 1830, Chlopicki is
appointed Dictator. On the 24th of December, 1830, Nicholas
issues a manifesto from St. Petersburg against the Poles. Austria
and Prussia are up in arms against the Poles. On the 5th of
January, 1831, the Poles issue a proclamation encouraging the
Revolution. On the 10th of January they make an open declaration
of their sufferings, setting forth how the Constitution was infringed
upon. On the 14th of February, 1831, the Russians are defeated
by the Patriots at the battle of Praga, with the loss of several
cannon. On the 19th and 20th of February, 1831, the battle of
Wawer takes place, without victory on either side. Skrzynecki
succeeds Chlopicki in the command of the Polish army. On the
25th of February, 1831, the battle of Grochow is fought, which
lasted until night; and although the Russians received a reinforce-
ment of 20,000 men, the Poles defeated them in many points on
this memorable and hard-fought day. The Poles under Skrynecki
were victorious in the battles of Igania, Ostrolenka, and Dembe.
The Polish General Dwernicki was surprised in a fog by the
Russians on the banks of the Bug, when his band of Patriots was
surrounded on all sides by the Russians. General Jankowski was
defeated by the Russians on the banks of the Vistula. The
Generalissimo Skrynecki wavers in his plan of action against the
Russians, and permits them without opposition to cross the Vistula.
Skrynecki is dismissed, and Dembinski appointed his successor.
The Russians attacked the fortress of Wola : the Patriots bravely
defended the place under the valiant Sowinski, when it was at last
taken. Generals Bem and Malachowski in a gallant manner
attempted to retake Wola, but were overpowered by numbers of

the enemy. After several other sanguinary encounters, the Patriots were compelled to surrender on the 5th of October, 1831. Thus ended this glorious effort to obtain the Freedom of Poland.

On the 30th of August, 1832, by the aggressive policy of Nicholas, Greece was separated from Turkey, when it was erected into a kingdom *dependent* on Russia. Otho II., son of the King of Bavaria, was proclaimed King. A war between Egypt and Turkey takes place by the Pasha Mehemit Ali invading Syria (1). In 1832 the Turks are defeated at the battles of Beylam, Aleppo (2), Damascus(3), and Koniah (4). Nicholas, apprehensive at the success of Mehemit Ali, offers to assist the Sultan, when he obtains from him the Treaty of Unkiar-Skelessi (5), dated June 26th, 1833. One of the articles in said Treaty, in favour of Russian supremacy in the Euxine, was to the effect that the Dardanelles were to be closed to the exclusion of all foreign vessels of war. France and England were opposed to said Treaty. On the 15th of July, 1840, the Treaty of London was signed between England, Russia, Prussia, and Austria, which had in view the security of the Ottoman Empire as a guarantee for the peace of Europe, and said Treaty nullified that of Unkiar-Shelessi. On the 13th of July, 1841, a further Treaty, to the same effect, was signed in London on behalf of France. Russia constantly engaged in war with the independent people of Caucasus, without acquiring any material extent of territory in that quarter, from the heroic devotion of the Circassians to their country in repelling Russian aggression.

On the 17th of February, 1846, Cracow throws off the tyrant's fetters, and establishes an independent government of its own on the 22d of February. The Polish Patriot, Count Patelsky, with a few followers, frightens Collin, the Austrian General,—the latter retiring from Cracow as the former enters. The Russians and

(1) Syria (with Palestine), an extensive Division of Turkey in Asia, bounded on the N. by the Amanian mountains, E. by the Euphrates and the Arabian desert, S. by Arabia Petræa, and W. by the Mediterranean Sea; area, 50,000 sq. m.; lat. 31° and 37° N., lon. 34° 30′ and 40° E.
(2) Aleppo (Haleb-es-Shabba), Chalybon and Beræa, a City of Turkey in Asia, in the N. of Syria, on the Koeik, 70 m. E. of the Mediterranean; lat. 36° 11′ N., lon. 37° 10′ E.
(3) Damascus (Es-Sham), a celebrated City of Syria, E. of Anti-Libarus, and 53 m. E.S.E. Beyrout; lat. 33° 27′ N., lon. 36° 23′ E.
(4) Koniah (or Koniyeh, Iconium), a City of Asia Minor; lat. 37° 51′ N., lon. 32° 40′ E.
(5) Unkiar-Skelessi, a Village of Asia Minor, on the Bosphorus, 8 m. N.N.E. of Constantinople.

Prussians, however, join the Austrians, when these Triumvirate forces surround Cracow, which soon falls into their hands. In the month of December 1846, in violation of the Treaty of Vienna, which guaranteed the independence of Cracow, this last remnant of ancient Poland is annexed to Austria.

On the 23rd of February, 1848, the French Revolution breaks out, when Louis Philippe retires to England, and a Republican Government is established in Paris. An insurrection breaks out in Bucharest; and on the 31st of July, 1848, Nicholas issues a cunningly-devised manifesto, appearing in conjunction with and as the ally of the Sultan, having for its alleged object, as stated therein, of " DEFEATING ANY EFFORT" that might be made by the Moldavians or Wallachians " TO IMPAIR THE INTEGRITY OF THE OTTOMAN EMPIRE, NOW MORE ESSENTIAL THAN EVER TO THE MAINTENANCE OF GENERAL PEACE!" It was then agreed upon that Russia should occupy for a period of five years the Principalities of Moldavia and Wallachia!

Hungary, after a long state of apathy, at length caught the flame of insurrection, and awoke into life! In May 1849, the Diet of Debreczin (1) issued its declaration of independence, which Hungary was a stranger to since 1711, when the civil wars at that period brought this independent nation within the grasp of Austrian domination, at which time Austria and Hungary became united under the control of one Sovereign. But the power of the Emperor of Austria was limited by the Hungarian Diet, the privileges of which that despot attempted to annihilate by recent innovations, when this oppressed country made a struggle to free itself from Austrian control, and to establish, as formerly, an independent kingdom under the ancient and illustrious house of Hapsburg. The Hungarians took up arms in defence of their just and legitimate rights, joined by the Polish Patriots, numbering 25,000 men, under Generals Bem and Dembinski. That upright and unsullied man, the noble Louis Kossuth, was raised by the Diet to the office of Governor or Dictator of Hungary; and that Traitor, General Georgey, was raised to the rank of Generalissimo over the Magyar and Polish forces. After the most brilliant encounters that the

---

(1) Debreczin, a royal free Town of E. Hungary, and, next to Pesth, the largest in the Kingdom, 116 m. E. of Pesth.

page of history ever recorded, and successes more triumphant than ever redounded to the credit and glory of a nation against the united forces of Austria and Russia, when victory after victory followed in rapid succession, until at length the course of Patriotism is stayed by the malignant blight of Treason and Treachery in the person of the General-in-Chief!—in the person of Georgey the Traitor! At the highest pinnacle of military glory, when the Russian soldiers let fall their fire-arms and knapsacks, and fled in consternation before the all-prevailing Patriots, the Russian General Rüdiger found an opening to the base, abandoned, and penurious principles of Georgey, who betrayed his friends, his country, and his countrymen, for the blighted and withering pestilence of Russian Gold! This Traitor gave orders that all the Generals under his command should yield to Russia. The towns of Peterwardien (1) and Arad (2) obeyed this wretch; but Klapka, the brave defender of Comorn (3), refused to obey this mandate, and held out till the 28th of September, 1849, when he was obliged to capitulate with the Russian and Austrian forces that surrounded this devoted place. Thus ended the struggle for Hungarian Freedom so gloriously commenced, but how treacherously compromised! The honourable, the virtuous, the noble Kossuth, who doubted the sincerity of Georgey, and who was opposed to the supreme command being entrusted into his hands, retired from Hungary with a troubled mind and oppressed heart; and mourning over the misfortunes of his country, which fell suicidal from the hands of one of its faithless children, that true Patriot, Louis Kossuth, went into exile.

The accession of Louis Napoleon to the Presidency of the French Republic is followed by his being proclaimed Emperor, when the different nations of Europe acknowledge him under such title. The Emperor Nicholas renews his old war against the Turks by invading the Danubian Principalities. The English and French Governments join in an alliance with the Turks against Russia, and pass the Dardanelles into the Euxine with their respective fleets; and on the 17th of September, 1854, the allied armies invade the Crimea, where were fought against the Russians—on the 20th, the battle of

---

(1) Peterwardien (Hung. Petervar), Capital of Slavonia, and the most formidable Fortress on the Danube, 44 m. N.W. Belgrade.
(2) Arad (Germ. Neu-Arad), a Town of Hungary on the Sharos.
(3) Comorn or Komorn, a royal free Town of Hungary on the Danube, 48 m. W.N.W. Buda.

Alma; on the 25th of October, the battle of Balaklava; on the 5th
of November, 1854, the battle of Inkerman; and on the 17th of
March, 1855, the battle of Eupatoria. On the 2nd of March, 1855,
the Emperor Nicholas departs this life, when he is succeeded by
his eldest son Alexander II.

O, my Friends and Brother Patriots! how can we lift our eyes from
that long catalogue of **Russian Barbarity!** without feeling
intensely for the cause of Poland!—without feeling intensely for
the cause of HUMANITY and FREEDOM all over the World!

Patriots, arise! Brothers and Friends of Freedom, awake, and
be no longer silent! Shake off the indolence of years, and be no
longer sluggards in the cause of Freedom! Hear me, the cause of
Poland is the cause of Europe! The Slavery of Poland is the
Bondage of the World! To those who may think otherwise, and
who are in the habit of indulging in the thought that "Britons
never will be Slaves," I would beg to refer their attention to the
traditional policy of Russia, and to what an extent the **Will!** of
Peter the "Great" has been, and may yet be carried out.

It may be well for us to consider the circumstances which gave
rise to, and under which that **Will!** was written, that we may be
the better able to judge of its authenticity, as we meet with some who
are so lost in wonder at its *fatal verification!* that they *doubt* its origin.

On referring to the History of Poland, we find that after the
HEREDITARY and PROSPEROUS Dynasties of Piast and Jagellon, com-
mencing in the year of Our Lord 830, and ending in the year 1572,
that anomaly of an **Elective Monarchy!** crept in, when
foreign Princes were eligible to compete for the Crown of Poland.
The many evils that sprung from this fatal privilege is too pondrous
a subject to treat of here: suffice it to say that it was the **Ruin of
Poland!** and the source from whence every other abuse flowed.

On traversing the period from 1576 to 1654, we meet with that
wild race of people denominated "COSSACKS" or "PLUNDERERS,"
the inhabitants of the Ukraine or frontier country, and during which
period they were enlisted in the cause of Poland, when, by reason
of some mismanagement of the Polish nobles and their elected
King Wladislas VII., the POLISH COSSACKS revolt! and attach

themselves to Russia in 1654, when Alexis, the father of Peter the " Great," was Czar of Russia. The ambition of Alexis is stirred up by this new alliance, when he invades Poland under a mere pretext, and marches two armies, composed of Cossacks and Muscovites, on Smolensko and Kio, and devastates the whole extent of Eastern Poland or Lithuania; when Severia and the Ukraine are ceded to Russia by the fatal Treaty of 1667.

Another evil that emanated from the Elective Monarchy was the disposition to engage in FOREIGN COMMOTIONS; whereas, if the Monarchy were HEREDITARY, there would be a far greater inclination on the part of the Sovereign to attend to the INTERNAL welfare of his own kingdom and that of his successors. But, by that baneful system of inviting *foreign Princes* to be partakers in the Regal dignity of the Polish Throne, avarice and corruption sprung up; the Candidates having no interest in the prosperity of Poland, looking merely for self-aggrandisement in the false and transient glitter of a purchased crown. As an instance of that pernicious system of foreign warfare, we have only to look at the reign of the Swedish Prince Sigismund III., elected King of Poland in 1587. We find this Monarch involving the Polish nation in a hurtful war with the Turks. Then he invades Russia, takes Moscow, captures the Czar, and brings him prisoner to Warsaw. There is no doubt that if Sigismund could have taken advantage of his victories, and turned them to some account, it would have materially altered the case; but it was otherwise, as it has invariably been the case with the long line of foreign conquests Poland has had the misfortune to obtain through the unprecedented valour of her sons! History informs us that Peter the " Great" never forgot the capture of Moscow and the bondage of his predecessor.

Another evil of the Elective System arises when the foreign candidate has OTHER INTERESTS that concern him SEPARATE from the Kingdom of Poland. On the death of his father, Sigismund III., as heir to the Crown of Sweden, seeks to become King, and drags the Polish nation into a three years' war with Sweden, ending in the total defeat of Sigismund by Adolphus Gustavus, when the territory of Livonia and part of Prussia is given up in 1629. However, in 1635, on the death of Adolphus Augustus, the Poles regain possession of this territory, but lose it afterwards. A similar but greater evil arises in the reign of Casimir III., who also lays

pretensions to the Crown of Sweden, but is opposed by Charles
Gustavus, who marches at the head of 60,000 troops into Poland, and
enters Warsaw. The fact of Charles Gustavus marching unopposed
and victorious through Poland is to be attributed the **cause of the
after aggression of Russia on Sweden;** for the
Czar Alexis, who at that time had invaded Poland in search of conquest, became jealous of Charles, withdrew his troops, and declared
war against Sweden. The result of this Swedish invasion of Poland
was most disastrous in its consequences, not alone to the future
welfare of Sweden, but to that of Poland. By the fatal Treaty of
Oliva on the 3rd of May, 1660, between Poland, Sweden, and
Prussia, Livonia is ceded to Sweden, and part of Prussia to the
Elector of Brandenburg (1). It was on this occasion that Poland
was endangered by a meditated partition-plot, when Sweden, Prussia,
and Austria, were to have been the participators! When we look
to the period of that great Polish General John Sobieski, the hero
of Chocium and a hundred fights! we LOOK IN VAIN for the WELFARE
of Poland under such victories! Here a Turkish, there a Cossack
encounter. The blood of Poland's Sons drench the foreign field of
battle when the hard hand of necessity obliges the formation of the
Pospolite or Polish Militia. Sobieski, by reason of his military valour,
is called upon to supply the place of the departed Wiecnowiecki,
and is elected King on the 19th of May, 1674. He defeats the
Turks at the battles of Leopol and Trembowla. Against the future
peace of Poland, Sobieski forms a *fatal* alliance with Austria. In
May 1683, the memorable siege of Vienna commences by the Turks
and Tartars. The months of May, June, July, and August, pass
over, and Vienna is about to yield to the invaders, when the strong
hand of the Polish King and General, at the head of 24,000 Poles,
comes to the rescue on the 12th of September, and John Sobieski
vanquishes the enemy, thereby SAVING AUSTRIA AND EASTERN
EUROPE!

Alas! for Poland, that day was one of those gloomy days that
spread the sepulchral shroud of **Europe's black ingratitude** which was to fold around the lifeless form of after-Poland,

---

(1) The Elector of Brandenburg, or Duke of Prussia, at the Treaty of
Wehlau, on the 19th of September, 1657, secured the independence of Ducal
Prussia, which was not made a kingdom of until 1701, when one of his
descendants, in the person of Frederick I., received the title of King of
Prussia.

and entomb her Freedom!   What the advantage gained?   Oh! my
heart sickens at the thought:—empty titles!   The forced and un-
willing compliments of European Kings and Princes were all the
reward that Sobieski and poor flattered Poland had to receive!
Listen to what the historian Rulhière says on this achievement of
the Polish arms:—

"This famous *deliverance* of invaded Germany became a CONTINUAL
SOURCE OF TROUBLES: not only had it *given rise to a war which the
Republic was not in a state to carry on, but it also* produced an
ALLIANCE which eventually *became* MORE FATAL *than the war
itself!*"

The alliance referred to by the historian was that formed with
Russia by Sobieski, who,—weakened and dispirited by successive
encounters with the Turks, and troubled with domestic dissensions,
—on the 6th of May, 1686, concludes a Treaty with the Czar, Peter
the "Great," by which he made a conveyance of Smolensko,
Czerniéchow, Kiow, and Severia, which had only been provisionally
conveyed in a former reign.   As the final stroke to all his victories,
John Sobieski departs this life on the 17th of June, 1696, leaving
Poland defenceless, and at the **mercy of the invader!**

The foregoing are the circumstances that gave rise to, and upon
which Peter the "Great" formed his ambitious projects so glaringly
manifest in the production he has thought proper to give to the
world in the form of his last **Will** and Testament, exhibiting, as
it does, the foul spirit of Anti-Christian spleen!   When we look at
this document, we are struck with the remarkable fact that Poland
is selected by him as the FIRST POINT! against which this aggressive
spirit is directed; and as the CENTRAL POINT, let us bear in mind,
from whence all other aggression is to radiate in the vast periphery of
after-conquest!   There is no doubt that if Peter the "Great" had
not gained a footing in Poland, he would never have penned, much
less thought of, such a production.   In Rule IV., on Poland, he
directs his successors to maintain " **The influence in the
country and at the Elections.**"   The influence in the
country the foregoing circumstances point out; while the influence
at the Elections of the King (Peter well knowing the *vulnerable* part
to strike the dart) is answered by what followed after the victory at
Pultowa, when Peter reinstates Augustus the Elector of Saxony on

the Polish Throne. His next aggression we find directed against
Sweden, in Rule V.; the circumstance which gave rise thereto being
already referred to. Under Rules VIII. and IX. we find this
monster, in his gloated avarice, taking a wide range of the World's
territory, from the Baltic to the Euxine, and from thence to the
confines of India, in Asia. In Rule X. we find this sacrilegious
fiend muttering something about "SPIRITUAL SUPREMACY" for the
furtherance of the "ORTHODOX FAITH!" Rules XI. and XII.
contemplate the subjugation of the World, when " **Russian
Arms will first inundate Germany, then
France, and in this way Europe will and
must be conquered!**"

Think not, my Brothers, that this last sentence of vile and black
atrocity is a mere vain or idle threat! Look at that **WILL** again—
read it—mark it—study it. "Subjugated Poland," "Vanquished
Sweden," the occupation of the Baltic and the Euxine Seas, &c. &c.
tells a woful tale! Are we to lie down in silent apathy, and await
the invader at our very doors? Are we to look in false dependence
on our Giant Fleet, so boasted as the "Wooden Walls of England,"
when Gallia bends beneath the Tyrant's Yoke and runs in streams
of blood? Are we to look in confidence at the narrow channel
that divides us from invaded Europe? Are we to await the dire
and mournful day when birds of prey will blight our path and
nestle in the land? Are we to see our very homes invaded; our
wives, the partners of our bosom, torn from our breasts? Are we
to witness our aged and honourable fathers trampled in the dust?
Are our noble mothers, who watched and cared us in our youth,
to be insulted? Are our fair daughters and sisters to be ravished
by a savage tribe? Are our infant darlings to be smothered in their
cradles? Are our pillaged homes to be set on fire? And many
such questions we may indeed and in truth ask ourselves. Methinks I hear some easy-going, never-thinking, money-making
Englishman reply, " O, tut, tut! nonsense, man! nonsense, man!
such can never take place." But "*such*," my quiet-going Friend,
will take place—if not in our own immediate day, at least in our
children's time. And what are all the riches we bequeath to those
we leave behind, if Russian pillagers divide the horded spoil?
"*Such*" devastation, I repeat again, *will take place*, unless we stem
the rapid torrent of aggression by rising at once and for ever in

DEFENCE OF POLISH NATIONALITY. All Cities! Towns! Villages! Hamlets! Streets! Lanes! Alleys! and Houses!—the Inhabitants of all!—Men, Women and Children, Lords and Peasants, Rich and Poor—SHOULD FEEL for the Cause of Poland! For it is the CAUSE of England, Ireland, and Scotland! For it is the CAUSE of France! For it is the CAUSE of Hungary and Freedom all over the World! Has not this **WILL** been carried out in its most material features? A careful glance at the foregoing EPITOME will answer in the affirmative. Well may we ask, *has the World been slumbering* for the last 130 years while that black cloud hung pendent with its iron sceptre over our heads? Had Britain's Flag, that "braved the battle and the breeze a thousand years," been furled? Had Gallia's valiant sons laid down their arms? Had Scotia and Hibernia slept? If so, ye Sons of Freedom, Awake!—Arise!—Shake off your Shame! The Alarm Bell sounds the note of War! Buckle on in Freedom's proud defence, and rid the World of a Tyrant! Regain the lost possessions of our Polish and Hungarian Brothers!

There is one barrier, however, in our way in getting more directly at Poland, which is Germany. The German States, thirty-eight in number, are more than Semi-Russian, Prussian, and Austrian, which Powers no doubt, though covertly, exercise an indirect control. Our first course of procedure should be to unite all the *irresponsible States* together under ONE HEAD, and establish, as formerly, an Emperor or King of Germany under a FREE CONSTITUTION, when either as an *ally* or a *foe* we could ascertain his intentions towards Russia; but in the present position of Germany, DIVIDED or PARTITIONED into so many petty Princedoms, having *separate* rights, and acting under NO ACKNOWLEDGED authority or head, we look in vain for SYMPATHY or open CANDOUR! This state of things must not, and cannot be allowed much longer. If the very HEART and CORE of EUROPE is allowed to ROT in this manner, the WHOLE must soon decay and wither beneath the blighting blast of Russian Despotism! A Prime Minister (1) of ours can tell us, as an

(1) "With respect to POLAND, I have no hesitation in stating **my own opinion**! that the Kingdom of Poland, as at present constituted, and as at present occupied, is a **standing menace to Germany**! It is for **the Powers of Germany to determine**! how far they may think that constitution of Poland is or is not dangerous to them, and whether, under circumstances which may lead them into a war with Russia, they will think it for their interests to endeavour to change that position of affairs!!—*Lord Palmerston, House of Commons, Tuesday, 20th March: extracted from the Times of Wednesday, 21st March,* 1855.

excuse for not interfering on behalf of Poland, that the more direct interests concerned in the Russian occupation of Poland is that of the Germanic States, when he well knew, as at present constituted, the Germanic States form a part and parcel of **Austro-Russian Policy!** and would be the **last to interfere!** in disturbing the Russian occupation of Poland. As to this Russian influence among the Germanic States, we see at once the source from whence it emanated when we direct our attention to Rule III. of the **Will** of Peter the "Great:"—"Russia is, on all possible occasions, to *intermeddle* in EUROPEAN DIFFERENCES, and affairs of *all kinds!* in particular, however, she is to do so in **those which concern Germany, on account of the proximity and more direct interest which is to be attached to that Country!"** If that desired object, the reconstruction of Germany, could be effected, and which it is the duty of every Patriot and Friend to Freedom to obtain in the furtherance of Poland, there could be no doubt as to its exercising a beneficial effect in WEAKENING the Triumvirate Powers. There is ONE FACT, and that an *important* one, which we should bear in mind as exhibiting to us the *influence* exercised by Russia and Austria in Germany :—the Germanic Confederation of 1815 emanated from that prolific source, the Vienna Congress, termed **"the Holy Alliance!"** by which the whole of the States formed an alliance to secure the integrity of the laws, and their several territories ; but which Germanic Confederation, however, became **dissolved** after the French Revolution of 1848, when Russia and Austria, apprehending a revolt of the Confederation, interfered by Nicholas of Russia nominating (through the Diet) John Archduke of Austria to the position of Vicar, Regent, or Viceroy of the Empire, with the proviso, however, to hold the same *under the supreme influence of the Czar*, and in which office the Archduke was installed on the 12th of July, 1848, by the **Traitorous Diet!** which held its last and seventy-first sitting! It is for the Governments of England and France to see (if they have not considered it before this) how far the Congress of Vienna was infringed upon by the total subversion to this guarantee to the independence of Germany ; or it may be that those Governments have given their consent thereto by a tacit compliance with this unconstitutional change. If so, the burden of

oppressed Europe is left on our shoulders, and which, by the power
of our UNITY, which is STRENGTH,—and by the COURAGE OF OUR
PATRIOTISM, which is LIFE,—not forgetting to pray to the Father
and Giver of all good things to *bless and prosper our undertaking*, we
say, Forward, Patriots! forward! The God of Justice!—the God
of Freedom!—the God of Battles! is with us, and whom have we
to fear? If Germany had not been, since Peter the "Great's" time
in particular, under the nod and beck of Russia, why did not that
stubborn, indolent, crouching race arise to protect a neighbouring
State? Why did not Germany lift up her head in defence of noble,
glorious Freedom, to prevent the three successive plunderings and
FALL OF POLAND? The answer is manifest—Because of its Austro-
Russian and Prussian tendency! That **Black Ingratitude**
of "invaded" **Germany!**—the total disregard to her past
DELIVERANCE in the dazzling days of Sobieski—the page of history
must record as a wanton and a bitter insult, in mockery of the
nobler feelings of our nature!

Our next concern is to contemplate the vast geographical extent
that Poland attained under the HEREDITARY and PROSPEROUS
Jagellon Dynasty, and to consider how far it may be practicable to
restore that Kingdom to its ancient boundaries. Its latitudinal
extent reached from the Baltic in the North to Turkey in the South,
having a longitude from Russia in the East to Germany on the
West; comprising the denominations of Great Poland, Little
Poland, and Lithuania, with an area in magnitude MORE EXTENSIVE
THAN THAT OF FRANCE; having a population computed at from
15,000,000 to 20,000,000 souls!

Ah! Friends of Freedom, is that mighty Nation to be swept
away from off the Earth,—shorn of the glorious beams of former
greatness nursed in the lap of Liberty,—without one trace or single
landmark to denote its past position? Is Tyrant Russia to engulf
within its wide expanse the far-extending territory of former Poland,
and immerse the millions of her Sons in Slavery? Say *not*, ye
Western Sons of Liberty! Say *not*, ye brave—ye resolute! Open
wide the arms of FRATERNAL LOVE, and share the sighs—the tears—
the heartfelt anguish of our suffering Brothers! Fold them in your
fond embrace, press them to your heart of hearts, feel THEIR
MISFORTUNE AS YOUR OWN! and *then*, and *not till then*, a brighter

day will mark the era of their FUTURE GLORY!—when Friendship's kindling rays will penetrate the mists, the clouds, the night of Despotism! and "DRIVE INVASION TO ITS NORTHERN DEN!" (1)

Our next consideration brings us in view of the relationship or *non*-relationship that existed between Russia, Prussia, and Austria, before the FIRST PARTITION of Poland took place in 1772. On consulting the foregoing Epitome, we find that under the reign of the Empress Elizabeth of Russia, and Frederick the "Great" of Prussia, war was carried on between these two Powers which did not terminate until the accession of the Czar Peter III., who became the ally of Prussia, and withdrew his troops. And, on consulting history, we find that Maria Theresa of Austria was an inveterate enemy of Russia, and more particularly under Catherine II., for whom Maria Theresa entertained a most marked dislike, calling Catherine by no other name than "that woman." However, through the mediation of Prussia, Kaunitz, her Minister, and Joseph II. her Son, Maria Theresa was constrained to listen to and entertain the iniquitous project of PARTITIONING POLAND! in league with Russia and Prussia: thereby uniting that Triumvirate Band of Spoliators, whose baneful influence completed the RUIN of unhappy Poland!

Mark well the FACT, my Brothers, that SUBJUGATED POLAND was the channel through which FORMER ENEMIES! became UNITED into SWORN ALLIES, thereby combining the DISUNITED DESPOTISM! of three Powers into ONE VAST WHOLE! against the future Peace and Happiness of Europe! Let us also bear in mind that, to RESTORE Peace and Happiness to Europe, we must SEPARATE, as formerly, Russia, Austria, and Prussia, by the RECONSTRUCTION OF POLAND! To REGAIN Poland, as also Hungary,—a consequent result thereon,—we must put from our thoughts all **Political tampering!** To pursue our object with SUCCESS, we must KNOW our ENEMIES from our FRIENDS! and not seek under the **subtle mantle** of **"Expediency!"** to give in **"there"** or give in **"here."** Our course must be one UNIFORM and UNDEVIATING PATH of DUTY! looking neither to the **"right hand"** nor to the **"left;"** pushing on with the indomitable WILL OF PATRIOTISM, though difficulties may

(1) See Kosciusko's address to his soldiers and fellow-countrymen. Act i. scene iv. page 21.

mountain-like rise to intercept us ; still, we will push on, trusting in
our GOD ! trusting in the GLORIOUS cause of FREEDOM that we are
engaged in ! till at length our UNITED EXERTIONS are crowned with
SUCCESS ! We denounce all **Alliance** with Austria and Prussia
as highly **dangerous** to the Cause of Freedom ! for they are
our tyrants as well as Russia. They also hold a part and parcel of
Polish Territory, from which we must EJECT them as **usurping
Tenants !**

It is now for us to consider how, under the eye of the then Free
Nations of Great Britain and France, the DISMEMBERMENT OF
POLAND was effected; and that the GOVERNMENTS of those countries
did not then raise their voice in defence of OPPRESSED LIBERTY !
As there is a mistake prevalent on this subject, in reference to the
non-interference of Great Britain, and which I feel it my duty to
correct, I will here give, in the form of a note, an extract from an
Address to Prince Czartorysky, "agreed to unanimously" at a
" crowded meeting," held in the Town Hall of Manchester, on the
evening of Monday, the 5th of March, 1855 (1). Although I join
altogether in the spirit and object of this noble Address, as being
the offspring of true Patriotism, nevertheless, it is my wish, in the
spirit of brotherly concern, to correct the statement that the former
"Apathy !" of Great Britain arose from " **the want of
proper knowledge of Foreign affairs !**" Such was
NOT THE FACT, as my Friends will perceive on consulting the foregoing Epitome ; or, to obtain a more enlarged view on this subject,
let them consult the Polish and Russian Historians. Such, my
Friends, I repeat, was NOT THE FACT ! The voice of Patriotism
was raised in England THEN as well as now, pleading on behalf of
Poland, and WARNING the Government of the day against
neglect ! but what was the result ?—the **same "Apathy !"**

---

(1) " We contemplate with poignant grief the *events of the past* which have
a reference to the melancholy fate of Poland.
" Her **Dismemberment** reflects a discredit upon the spirit of the
times ; but we chiefly deplore the **indifference !** with which Great Britain
beheld the consummation of that act of Spoliation !
" However, we are inclined to ascribe **that Apathy more to the
want of proper knowledge of Foreign affairs !** than to the
influence of unfriendly feeling.
" WE are now anxious to make a COMPENSATION ! for what we consider
to have been **a grave political error !** by the MANIFESTATION OF OUR
SYMPATHY, and a desire to support the claims of Poland to her NATIONAL
INDEPENDENCE !"

which we have so RECENTLY witnessed in Parliament! On referring to the *Self*-infliction—"WE are now anxious to make a COMPENSATION :"—As Patriots, we do ourselves an injustice by coupling the **fatal guilt!** of a **Government** with the EXERTIONS of our FORMER Patriotism on behalf of Poland! Let us bear in mind that whenever the SPIRIT of a GOVERNMENT (no matter what its PROFESSIONS! may be) is **anti-patriotic**, we should learn to discriminate between the Government and the PATRIOTIC INTENTIONS of the PEOPLE. If we couple the **Guilt** of the *former* with the INNOCENCE of the latter, we fall into an egregious error; and the **fatal mistake!** resulting from this is:— The People looking to the Government, in place of the Government having to look to the People!

The Government had full "knowledge of Foreign affairs!" so much so, that the English ambassador was a **Mendicant** at the Court of St. Petersburg, begging for **Naval Assistance** against France. It was not to be supposed, in compliance with the policy of **intrigue**, that the English Government, **well informed** on the **Partition Plot!** both before and after its consummation in the superlative degree! would have thought it "expedient" to have raised any opposition to the **intentions** of the Empress Catherine II., be those intentions ever so **iniquitous!** As a bait to lure away the faint shadow of any opposition on the part of the English Government to Catherine's designs on Poland, this artful woman **purchased** from that quarter the Freedom of Poland, by some promised " **commercial**" advantages! The boasted " **Glory**" of the long-lived reign of George III. sinks into contemptible insignificance and **appalling depravity!** when we behold the **ruin** that monarch and his ministers have sanctioned, in the **Downfall of Poland!**

Methinks I hear some defender of the boasted " Glory!" of other days reply:—"Come now, you are too severe; you seem to forget the long wars with France and America, when all our disposable forces were engaged; so that, if we were even inclined to assist the Poles, we could not, in a military point of view." True, there is something tangible in that remark; ard I must admit this friend of boasted " Glory!" has gained a point. However, if military aid was not at hand to rescue Poland, why be partaker in the plot, and not recall the British Ambassador at the Russian Court? No

e

doubt the old war between England and France was the source of
many evils, and Catherine well knew that. Although that prolific
Will! of Peter the "Great!" does not imply in exact terms by
naming England and France in reference to what he lays down in
Rule V. as to Sweden and Denmark, between whom "a feeling
of jealousy is to be constantly kept up!" nevertheless, we read in
Rule III. that **"Russia is on all possible occasions to intermeddle in European Differences
and affairs of all kinds!"** And it is well known, as
history informs us, that the intermeddling of Russia had a great
share in promoting the long war between England and France.
There was a constant scene of intrigue carried on from time to time
at the Court of St. Petersburg between the English and French
Ambassadors, one acting against the other, who would alternately
advise with the Empress Catherine II. as to the hostile designs
formed by England against France, and *vice versâ*,—much to the
flattered vanity and gloated satisfaction of that Tyrant!

Napoleon I. made some exertions to restore the independence of
Poland ; and, no doubt, if he had succeeded in the Moscow expedition, he might have accomplished more for that kingdom ; but his
misfortunes on that occasion had weakened him and the Poles too
much, to be ever after of any assistance in securing the Nationality
of Poland,—unless we are to conjecture what might have taken
place had Napoleon been successful at the Battle of Waterloo. If
we may judge of Napoleon's feelings (1) expressed (on the eve of his
departure for Russia) to the Polish Deputation that waited on him
at Wilna on the 26th of June, 1812, we must see in that great but
unfortunate man, a Friend, or professed Friend, to the Nationality
of Poland. However, Napoleon's reply to the Deputation in other
respects was ambiguous ; nor was his allusion to Austria retaining
possession of her share in the plunder of Poland at all acceptable to
the national representatives. No doubt Napoleon's MATRIMONIAL
ALLIANCE with the House of Austria had much to do in giving
expression to such a sentiment.

---

(1) "If I had reigned at the time of the FIRST, SECOND, or THIRD
PARTITION OF POLAND. I would have ARMED ALL MY PEOPLE TO SUPPORT
YOU! I LOVE your nation; during the last sixteen years I have seen your
soldiers at my side in the fields of Italy, as well as those of Spain. I
APPLAUD ALL THAT YOU HAVE DONE! I SANCTION THE EFFORTS YOU
WISH TO MAKE! I WILL DO EVERY THING IN MY POWER TO SECOND
YOUR RESOLUTIONS!" &c. &c.

It is a remarkable fact—and one that I would impress upon my Brother Patriots the importance of DWELLING ON—that the Crown of Poland hung suspended over the wide plains of Waterloo until the result of that memorable battle was known, when Alexander I. of Russia **two days after** (on the 20th of June, 1815) **had himself crowned King of Poland!** (see Epitome). And that battle, misnamed the Battle of "**Deliverance!**" was to the Poles the battle that decided their further and final state of Slavery! and endangered the future peace of Europe in furthering the ambitious designs of the Russian Autocrat! If I were to follow the bent of my inclination, and give way to the rapid succession of thoughts pregnant with facts! that crowd upon my mind while I pen these lines, I would have much to say suggestive of deep and impor- tant matter on this remarkable era in the History of the World! but satisfying myself that with your knowledge of history, and RETENTIVE MEMORY, similar suggestions and convictions may strike your Patriotic minds, I forego this arduous task, leaving it in your hands to supply my deficiency, being anxious to hurry on to matters within our own immediate time.

The Government of this country has ever been the **Govern-ment** of "**Expediency!**" the chameleon character of which is ever ready to form such a diversity of colour that we look in vain for the UNCHANGEABLE CONSTITUTION of a Free Nation, not alone in a domestic sense, but more especially in regard to its relationship with Foreign Countries. As an illustration of this fact in a FOREIGN point of view, I will here give one out of many such cases :—We find, on the visit of the Emperor Nicholas to England in 1844, when (*let us bear in mind*) Louis Philippe was on the French throne, that there was a secret negociation carried on *in propriâ personâ* between Nicholas on the one hand, and some members of a then and future Government on the other, having reference to a medi- tated Russian Invasion of the Turkish Empire, which resulted in the **entire approbation!** (through *fear*, however!) of certain gentlemen whose names it is unnecessary now to mention! We then find this chameleon Government appearing in a *different* hue after the French Revolution in 1848, and siding with the Emperor Napoleon III. against Russia, after the meditated Turkish Invasion, planned and agreed upon in 1844, had actually taken place! How- ever, it may be necessary to remark here the fact, that, had Louis

Philippe still occupied the throne of France, as in 1844, Nicholas had had full scope to put forth with impunity his aggressive designs against Turkey, as far as the English Government was concerned ; and as it is well known that Louis Philippe had made a similar engagement with Russia, and which object in view no doubt hastened the overthrow of that monarch by that discerning, free, and independent people of whom the French nation is composed.

We now arrive at a remarkable period in the History of the World, when we behold the union of two nations heretofore at war with each other, and whose armies are now combined for the suppression of Russian Aggression. Although I have said " the union of two nations," I have said so merely in a POSITIVE sense ; for I am not one of those sanguine creatures of the age, that fondles in his mind the **delusion** that there is really, and in a SUPERLATIVE degree, a lasting union between the British and French nations! Would that I could believe it! but the truth of the case is otherwise. To consider this point in its true character and meaning, we must draw the WIDE DISTINCTION that exists between the **Government of a Nation** and the NATION ITSELF! And although the French nation is more fully identified with her Government in the present day, still we cannot assert in truth that a similar identification holds good between the British Government and the British Nation. Then comes the point of the relationship that exists between the French and British Governments, which we must DISTINGUISH from the relationship or *non*-relationship existing between the French and British Nations ; for that Government relationship between the two countries in these perplexing days of **timid statesmanship!** may be productive of that Green-eyed Monster of " **Expediency !**" when matters of great national importance! may be " **compromised !**" for the sake of obtaining a present cessation from hostilities! Such compromise, let us bear in mind, would be a **Government** and NOT A NATIONAL **Compromise!** for who could suppose that that person who really understood the character of the British and French nations would for one moment assert, that the all-powerful and public voice of either country had given in its approval to any such **meditated Compromise** with Russia? Such a compromise, my Brother Patriots, it grieves me to confess, is now in progress, and no doubt will end, as all other Treaties have, on most advantageous terms to Russia; or, at least, so far in favour of that Power (on the contemptible "**Four Points !**"), and the Autocrat's vassals, Austria and Prussia, that a wide margin will be left for any evasion of the ominous terms of said Treaty, and which dereliction on their part will only serve as a further confirmation of Treaties formerly ignored, and to which they had affixed their **polluted** signatures !

As I am on this point, I cannot but notice one personage who has natural, but, I regret to say, for his own and his country's sake abused and misapplied abilities,—a recent "Envoy, Ambassador, Plenipotentiary Extraordinary, in cases of extreme moment and the utmost peril ! in matters which admit of no delay ! but require the utmost velocity and magnetic telegraphic haste !" &c. &c. &c., and whatever else the fears and apprehensions of some may designate him. Well, this Envoy, or whatever else we may choose to call him, has been recently deputed by that amalgamated community bearing the title of "**The British Government !**" to repair with the aforesaid accelerated pace to Vienna, under the far-fetched and delusive prospect, as that Minister states in his Address (dated from Paris, February 23, 1855) to the Electors of London, "**affording hopes** of an **honourable termination** of the present War !" And again he adds :—his "Mission" "**is that of the highest importance involving the interests of Europe !**" To comment on such bombast and contemptible vanity ! would, I conceive, be a further infliction on the patience of my friends; but leaving such sentiments, under such circumstances, to speak for what they are worth, I lay down my pen, concluding with the remark that this is the statesman who asserted—"**I do not desire to take away one inch of territory from Russia !**"

There is one word of advice which I think it my duty to give my friends :—Keep and carry about with you a Pocket Political Diary alphabetically arranged, containing the *Dramatis Personæ* of the Tragic Political Farce of certain would-be statesmen who make their *entrée* on the stage of both Houses of the Legislative Assembly : mark well, in an abstract form, the "sayings and doings" of each Actor, and depend upon it you will find an heterogeneous mass of diversity ! and contrariety ! in each performer, as the political current may chance to drive him,—when you will behold, in the brief compass of a few years, that strange anomaly, the **same individual** contradicting himself on more than one or two occasions. In reference to this point, I will not give the exact contradictions of the Minister, as I cannot afford space for same, but will content myself with giving you in a note (1) another extract from the "sayings" of the Minister in question. After reading that extract, my Brothers, it cannot but suggest to your minds two palpable facts: The first is, that the "Government" had a **secret understanding** for some time back (as you may infer from the words **"all along known!"**) with the Austrian Government, concerning which the people of this country were kept in ignorance, until the expression of the Minister at that late hour gave it publicity! The next fact is the consequent **result** or **effect** of such a secret understanding carried out,—manifesting, on the part of the "Government!" of this Free Nation, a disposition and a determination **to uphold at all hazards the Austrian occupation of Hungary!** Would such sentiments, I ask, obtain for one moment that black and withering **"Hear, hear!"** in any Popular Assembly of the British Nation outside the **corrupted** (2) House of Commons? If there be any one so base, or so unjust to the Patriotic sentiments of the British Nation, as to give an affirmative to that interrogatory, I would tell such an individual that he was a Slave, and the minion of Slavery!

It is now for us to consider the Truth or **Falsehood!** of the statement that it **"would be a Great Misfortune to Europe if Hungary were separated from the Austrian Empire;"** because Lord Palmerston **"con-**

(1) "The Austrian Government **know!** and have **all along known!** that the Government of Great Britain **would consider it a Great Misfortune to Europe if Hungary were separated!** from the Austrian Empire; because I consider the Austrian Empire as an aggregate Body in the Centre of Europe, to be an essential Element! in the Balance of Power in Europe!! The Austrian Government, therefore, have no Doubt! as to what are the Policy! and Views! of the Government in regard to Hungary!!! (Hear, Hear!)" — *Lord Palmerston, in the House of Commons, on Tuesday, 20th March, 1855. Extracted from the Times of Wednesday, the 21st of March, 1855.*

(2) When I say "corrupted House of Commons," I would not wish to be understood as implicating the whole of its members,—among whom there are some of the NOBLEST PATRIOTS!—However, there is a certain Class of individuals in that House who have not escaped observation, and it is to those individuals that I would apply the term "**Corrupted House of Commons**"! That "**Hear, Hear,**" I should hope and do believe was not general, but was confined to **that Class** who on that occasion represented in the public journals the House of Commons!

REMARKS. lv

**siders the Austrian Empire, as an aggregate
Body in the centre of Europe, to be an essential Element in the Balance of Power in
Europe!"** I can lay my hand to my heart and say, in the
most perfect sincerity, that there **never was a falser
statement!** from the lips of any Minister! The only excuse
I can make in palliation for such an avowal is, that the Minister
said so not knowing or considering what he said, or he was most
profoundly ignorant, or **thought his hearers so!** on the
results of the late Hungarian Revolution! My Brother Patriots,
what was the result of the late Hungarian War?—why, it has given
rise to the late Turkish Invasion by Russia, which has caused so
much bloodshed, not alone to Turkey, but to France, England,
Ireland, and Scotland, losses which I have no doubt it will take
years to recover! If the Hungarian Revolution had been successful
the late Emperor Nicholas of Russia would never have dared an
invasion of Turkey! If that noble feeling of Patriotism had been
successful, Poland would have ere this thrown off the Tyrant's
fetters, and would now be a Free Nation! If that glorious movement had been (but for the Traitor's hand) victorious, Russia,
Prussia, and Austria, would now be separated, and reduced to their
former insignificance among the nations of Europe! If that noble
Revolution had been successful, then, indeed, the "Balance of
Power" in Europe would have been consummated! We also
deduce from the foregoing maxim the apologist, or I should, more
correctly speaking, say the panegyrist, of the late Emperor Nicholas
in the person of the present Prime Minister of England! for *there*
a justification is set up of the **" intermeddling"** of Russia
as the ally of Austria, in putting an end to the Patriotic Movement
in Hungary, thereby, mind you, giving Russia the credit of establishing that **" Essential Element in the Balance
of Power in Europe!"** which " Balance," however, on
consulting the **Will!** of Peter the " Great" and the antecedents
of Nicholas, and his Grandmother Catherine II., has never been
the object or intention of Russia to promote, much less to maintain.

If that Glorious and immortal Revolution which panted for the
independence of Hungary as well as Poland was SUCCESSFUL! the
Hungarian as well as the Polish Ambassadors at the British Court
would ere this have been heaped with fulsome adulations without

number, by the very Minister and his clique who now plot and
connive with the oppressors of those noble countries! If the
French Revolution of 1848 was unsuccessful, the London obscurity
of Louis Napoleon, the present Emperor of the French, would
still continue ; and to imagine or suppose for one moment that the
runaway Prisoner of Ham and exiled Louis Napoleon would be
the guest at Buckingham Palace under the reign of the House of
Bourbon, would be to say that there was no corruption in Court
intrigue, or in the manner the national affairs of Great Britain were
controlled and attempted to be carried on! What is there to prevent another Revolution taking place in France, in the event of the
death of Louis Napoleon?—and what, may I ask, will be the result
or effect of such a Revolution upon this country as at present constituted? Supposing, for argument sake, the "Four Points!"
Treaty is concluded at Vienna ; the shattered armies return ; the
British and French Ambassadors resume their offices at the Court
of St. Petersburg, what then, may I ask, will be the upshot of such
a peace? Why the "**intermeddling**" so legibly pourtrayed in the **Will!** of Peter the "Great" and his successors
"**in European Differences and affairs of all
kinds!**" will be put into requisition again with a thousand-fold
force ; when England and France, the two powers that can only
guarantee the observance of said contemptible Treaty, will be set in
battle array against each other, when the Treaty, as a matter of
course, falls to the ground for want of its legitimate and allied
supporters ; — when the old spirit of exciting a feeling "**of
jealousy**" which "**is constantly to be kept up!**"
will revive with redoubled energy, when the Ambassadors of two
friendly Governments, in place of being the allied representatives
of Great Britain and France at the Court of St. Petersburg, will
become the medium or channel (as formerly) through which will
flow the antagonistic currents of the bitterest hatred and acrimony,
ending in producing the troubled agitation of strife, which may
shipwreck and engulf in one common whirlpool, not alone the freedom of Great Britain and France, but will drag along with it the
hopes and the expectations of a glorious Patriotism, which seeks
and aspires to the noble and manly task, of ridding Europe and the
World from the raging cataract of Despotism!

It affords us some relief, however, to be able to select out of the

incongruous mass of Statesmen one who (I would hope) is a
Patriot:—although youthful, Sir Robert Peel has a candid and
discerning mind far surpassing the acumen of much older Statesmen and would-be celebrities. How far his connexion with the
present Government may operate in forfeiting the sentiments he
has already given expression to on behalf of Poland and Hungary,
is yet to be ascertained; however, I would consider it an injustice
to that Right Honourable Baronet to identify him with the foregoing avowal of his colleague in office, if I was so negligent as not
to give here the noble sentiments which the mouth, and we should
fondly hope the heart, of Sir Robert Peel gave utterance to, the
spirit and truth of which every Patriot must admire :—" Russia
had again provoked a war, which he trusted might result in
RESTORING POLAND! to her position as a Nation, and give LIBERTY
to a people which had been so long **enslaved !**" (1). Again, on
another occasion :—" No settlement of the Eastern question would
be satisfactory UNLESS POLAND AND HUNGARY WERE RESTORED!
An **Austrian alliance** he denounced!" (2). Would that I
could print such sentiments, as they deserve, in gold letters; or
that I could present them placarded in Large Type before the
perpetual notice of Lord Palmerston!

We find the venerable Lord Lyndhurst giving a lengthened
oration in the House of Lords, on Monday, the 19th of March,
1855,—from which we deduce the *understood* yet *silent* anguish of
that nobleman, mourning as it were over the *incapacity* or *negligence*
of his early days, by not warning the *then* Government on behalf of
Polish Nationality ere it was *too late* of what that learned and aged
gentleman tells the *present* Government (a fact, however, with which
the Historical Student is conversant), was the " **aggressive
character of Russia**" under Peter I. and Catherine II. &c.;
and the " **Treachery**" of Prussia under the monarchs
Frederick the "Great," and Frederick William, his successor. I
have, however, in the name of Patriotism, to thank that noble and

(1) Sir Robert Peel, Bart., at Tamworth, January 1855, on the occasion of a
soirée, in connection with the Library and Reading-Room for the Working
Classes.
(2) Sir Robert Peel, Bart., at Tamworth, on Wednesday, March 15, 1855,
on the occasion of his being re-elected M.P. without opposition, after he had
accepted office as a Junior Lord of the Admiralty under Lord Palmerston
as Premier.—*Extract from the Times of Thursday, the* 15*th of March,* 1855,
being a correct and compared copy thereof.

learned Lord for introducing such palpable truths at this particular
time ; as it manifests a disposition in that nobleman to make some
amends for the *past*, by exhibiting (what he no doubt considered it
his duty) an unflinching determination on his part to " tell the
Truth, the whole Truth, and nothing but the Truth," in the face of
a **corrupt Administration,** and pending a contemptible
though **dangerous Treaty!**

We now come to consider a resolution that was proposed by that
true Patriot, Mr. P. A. Taylor, at a meeting held in the Guildhall,
on Saturday, the 3d of March, 1855, to elect a Member for the
City of London, in the room of Lord John Russell, who accepted
office under the Palmerston Ministry. After the Electors of London
had made the *sad mistake !* to re-elect that veritable personage, who
had taken his departure for Vienna, for the purpose of creating (as
he thinks) an imperishable name, (and under the impression of
insuring his re-election, bearing in his mind no doubt the poetic
reflection, that " Distance lends enchantment to the view"),
Mr. Taylor proposed the following Resolution :—" That, in the
opinion of this Meeting, no Treaty with Russia will be satisfactory
that does not enforce some material territorial clause." After an
able and eloquent address, which I regret I cannot insert here,
the Sheriffs refusing to put the Resolution, the Patriotic Mr. Taylor
put it himself, when it was carried by the unanimous voice of the
Meeting. The foregoing Resolution points out two courses for the
adoption of the Government :—1st, That there is to be " no Treaty ;"
2d, If a Treaty, a Territorial one, by which Russia should consent to
forego more or less (as the case might be) of the extensive plunder
to which the Autocrat lays claim. As to the *first* proposition, that
there is to be " no Treaty," I entirely concur ; as to the *second*, the
well-known policy of Russia is so utterly at variance, that we must
entirely discard it from our minds as futile. I will take for granted,
then, that said Resolution is one altogether on the " NO TREATY"
principle, and upon such offer a few remarks. After the Allied
Fleets entered the Euxine, and the Anglo-French Armies had
landed in the Crimea, from thenceforward there should have been
no **wavering** or going back on the " Four Points" or any other
number of points ; for by so doing, the Governments who preside
over the National affairs of Great Britain and France exhibit a
weakness which I consider **more dangerous** than the

Treaty now pending. For what does it do? It is just like making
a compact or agreement with a **Robber!**—that if he comes to
terms and accedes to "**so much!**" and "**no more!**" he is
at perfect liberty to "**retain the Plunder!**" he already
possesses, giving him full scope to **pillage ad infinitum!**
in all other directions! To admit the fact, that we are disposed to
come to terms with an **Outlaw!** is to make a confession that he
is **not that Outlaw!** we would suppose him to be, but one
who has seldom or never transgressed the boundaries of former
stipulations; and one in whose "**Good Faith!**" we may
place implicit confidence as a guarantee for the fulfilment of all
future engagements which may concern and **jeopardise the
honour and security of nations!**

As I am on the "No-Treaty" principle, I cannot, in justice to
Poland, overlook a statement conveyed in a Resolution (1) proposed
at a crowded Meeting held in the Guildhall of Bath, on Thursday,
the 15th of February, 1855, the Mayor, Mr. W. Hunt, presiding.
The Resolution, I am gratified to say, speaks for itself, and was
unanimously agreed to by that respectable and crowded meeting.
Comment on my part would be superfluous.

We must now consider by what infatuation the Governments of
England and France were led into the humiliating position of looking (after hostilities commenced) for a further negociation about
the "**Four Points.**" No doubt the pride of the two
Governments is a little crestfallen before the stubborn and unforeseen opposition of Russia, and, although that may have its weight,
nevertheless, the true secret of stipulation springs from Austrian
and Russian intermeddling, planning, concocting, proposing,
devising, &c. &c. &c. as the **secret Agents!** as well as
Vassals of Russia! To have an **Austrian** Ambassador
in London and another in Paris during the present war, is virtually
the **same** as if those identical personages were **Russian**

---

(1) " That the strongholds and armaments prepared by Russia in advance
of her ancient frontiers have revealed AGGRESSIVE PURPOSES, AGAINST
WHICH TREATIES ARE NOT EFFECTIVE DEFENCES, Russia having already
seized upon Territories since her first Partition of Poland in 1772 equal in
extent and importance to the whole Empire she possessed in Europe before
that period; that the RESTORATION OF POLAND! in COMPLETE INDEPEN-
DENCE of Russian control, would afford a material guarantee that Russian
aggrandizement in Europe at the expense of neighbouring States should
cease; and that such Restoration of Poland would be in accordance with
justice and sound policy."

Ambassadors! with this difference, however, that the former, although admitted **" Friends !"** are **dangerous Enemies!** spying out the "nakedness of the land;" observing and reporting through Vienna and Berlin, and from thence to St. Petersburg, the **weak and vulnerable** points of the two respective Cabinets. That system of communication kept up, no wonder there should be a **delay** in coming to an agreement on the "Four-Points" Treaty! now pending;—and we may expect a far more protracted Congress until the direct course is taken against such functionaries by the Governments of England and France ordering them to leave forthwith! Why should the Austrian Minister the other day controul the free expression of a Patriotic Statesman (1), as to force a **contrary avowal** from the lips of his colleague (2) in office, but for a certain **mysterious fear!** that hangs around the path of Ministers, in dread of an armed Austro-Russian combination. Paltry and **fallen!** is that Administration that bows, and stoops, and fawns in **craven servility** to the **will** and **threatenings of Tyrants!** and that pendant-like hangs on the **fatal** and **delusive Hopes!** that through such contrivances of low subserviency, the **" peace"!** and **" security"!** of Europe and the World will be obtained!

We now come to consider the position Napoleon III. and his Government stands in with respect to Austria and Prussia; and how far the Government of England is held within the **magnetic influence** that has its **gravitating Power** in the **Capital of France;** and in what direction, how far, and to what purpose or effect the **vacillating** wires of **intrigue** may move? This is an interrogatory upon which pages could be written in reply; but apprehensive that I have exceeded the limits originally prescribed for the Remarks as introductory to the Drama, I must check a mental impetuosity, and satisfy my Brothers with a simple reference to this subject. Napoleon I., the uncle of the present Emperor, intermarried with the House of Austria; and we

---

(1) Sir Robert Peel, Bart., at Tamworth, on Wednesday, the 15th of March, 1855.
(2) Lord Palmerston, in his place as Prime Minister, in the House of Commons, on Tuesday, the 21st of March, 1855, in answer to a question from Lord W. Graham, in reference to the Austrian Ambassador, and the views Sir Robert Peel held and expressed with regard to Poland and Hungary.

find that said **alliance influenced** in a great measure Napoleon's conduct towards Poland. In the present instance, such matrimonial Alliance does not exist; nor can we trace the ties of consanguinity from the Austrian Princes to the present Emperor. I refer to this merely to show that, while the Uncle might have feigned some plausible excuse for a leaning towards Austria, in that Power's occupation of Gallicia in Poland, still the Nephew could not put forward any such pretext.

Louis Napoleon and the French Government have given in their adhesion to the "**Four Points**"! by which, so far as that Government, (1) in conjunction with the Government of England, is concerned, will **bind** them "**neck and heels!**" NOT TO INTERFERE! in the re-establishment of Hungary and Poland, but **silently consenting!** to **leave** those countries **in the hands** of their present Rulers and **ungovernable Tyrants!** Although Ministers may treat us like "**fools**"! and think to quiet our anxiety about the welfare of our brothers in bondage, by telling us, as formerly, that Poland or Hungary is "**not mentioned**"! in said Treaty, it being for an entirely "**different object**"! still, unless we are downright idiots, we must see the bent of that **reply!** which tells us although Poland or Hungary is not stipulated for in said Treaty, which has for its professed object "**the restoration of Peace**"! yet, by reason of the **fatal silence!** on Poland and Hungary, **that silence!** makes an **open confession!** in the eyes of the World, of the Austro-Russian Prussian occupation of those countries, and their "**right**"! and "**title**"! thereto, "**now, and for ever after**"!—In reference to the policy of the French Government towards Prussia, it is evidently of an **undecided** character; whether hostile or friendly, it undoubtedly bears the aspect of **conciliation.** We learn, however, the following information from the "Times" Correspondent writing from Berlin on the 27th of February, 1855 :—

"The French proposal, that Prussia should conclude a second edition of the December Treaty, with some modifications, has been

---

(1) When I refer to such acts of the French Government in conjunction with the English Government, I would wish to be distinctly understood as not involving the honour of either nation. The argument I hold is, that free nations like Great Britain and France are not bound by the **misdeeds!** **or traitorous acts!** of **nominal Governments!**

f

rejected.   Prussia requires a **promise from France**, **that she will not march any troops through or into Federal territory, and that no attempt shall be made to insurrectionise Poland!** When these two points are conceded, Prussia is ready to sign a protocol with the Allies on the basis of the *aide-mémoire* of Dec. 28th, preparatory to entering upon the approaching Conferences at Vienna."(1) How far the Emperor Napoleon or his Government are likely to entertain such a proposition in reference to Poland, I cannot take upon myself to form any opinion ; but this much I may add in the way of a friendly admonition, that if **such a "promise"!** is exacted from Louis Napoleon and his government, and that he continues to act in **conjunction with Austria!** in opposition to any change in Hungary, the sooner he retires from the responsible position he now holds, the better ; for I well know the NATIONAL FEELING of France, as also that of Great Britain, will NEVER SUBMIT to such a line of policy, so **detrimental** to the security and liberties of Europe! If Louis Napoleon wants to secure his throne, he will at once and for ever declare himself the FRIEND OF LIBERTY! by throwing off the **doubtful and pernicious Austro-Prussian Alliance!** then will the French and British Nations greet him with one voice, as the Champion of the Liberties of Mankind, when they may well shout aloud " Vive l'Empéreur !" " Vive Napoléon !"

It was the baneful influence of the Austro-Prussian alliance with the Western Governments that led to, planned, and concocted that disastrous scheme, **The Invasion of the Crimea!** but for which a MORE DIRECT COURSE would have been taken against Russia by the Anglo-French armies crossing Germany and entering Poland and Hungary. It was the same to the Turks where the Russians would be attacked by the allied forces, so as that desired event took place ; and there can be no doubt that Poland and Hungary would have been the most advantageous ground upon which to commence and prosecute hostilities. Then, again, previous to the Anglo-French armies appearing in Poland and Hungary, the NATIONAL FEELINGS and SYMPATHY of those depressed countries

---

(1) Extracted from an article of the *Times* Correspondent, dated 27th of February, 1855, and appearing in the *Times* of Saturday, the 3rd of March, 1855. (*True and compared copy.*)

could have been appealed to, and still further awakened to a
LIVELY PATRIOTISM through their corresponding agents in these
countries, which would not fail to have had the desired effect.
That **semi-friendly, semi-threatening** system which
has been **interchanged** of late between the Governments
of England and France with the Austro-Prussian Governments, has been most **pernicious** in its effects! Valuable time
has not alone been sacrificed to such **political tampering,**
having for its author that Bugbear "**Expediency**"! the
source and fomenter of **many evils**! but the Western Governments have let slip, by such culpable folly, any probability that
there might have been of securing the peace of Europe. The Western
Governments have been held for some time back in complete
check! by the Austro-Prussian Governments, until the **ner-
vous susceptibility**! of the former has been so worked upon
by the **enervating influence** of the latter, that we may
now look upon the Western Governments as totally **incapable**
and **powerless** for any DECIDED ACTION against **Russian
aggression**! when we witness the result of such POLITICAL
TAMPERING in the **mortifying** and pitiable spectacle of that
"**Four Points**" Gangrene!

I regret to say that the time has gone by when the military development of the Western Governments could have shone forth
unto LONG and DURABLE victory, in attacking Russia in the RIGHT
DIRECTION; when the once splendid, but now **sadly depopulated** armies, engaged in a **fruitless expedition**! would
have gone forth in the valour of their might on the European
plains, hailed as CONQUERORS of **Russian Despotism**! and
DELIVERERS of not only the Turkish Empire, but also of the Polish
and Hungarian Nations! But how does the case now stand? Why,
up to the present time, the Western Governments, notwithstanding
the "**victories**"! and consequent **bloodshed** that has ensued,
have not, nor will they ever obtain, by such a procedure the independence and security of one of those Powers, but are now in
treaty on the **dastardly** "**Four Points**"! to the imminent
peril of all! For who is that individual, let him be ever so **sanguine** as to the probability of peace on the "**Four Points**"
Treaty, that could lay his hand upon his heart and solemnly declare
that he is satisfied therewith, but will on reflection exclaim, that

under such a proviso our "**last state!**" will be "**worse than the first!**"

Oh! that the Governments of Great Britain and France had paused awhile ere they took that **fatal** and **delusive step!** the **Crimean Expedition,**—fatal because of its **long** and **tedious course,** when **disease** and **death** had marked many a warrior for an **early tomb!** ere the din of battle was heard upon that **distant shore!** Oh! that the united Governments of Western Europe had called to the rescue such men, as the upright, noble, and illustrious Louis Kossuth and Prince Czartoryski! men whose NAMES are on the LIPS! and TREASURED in the HEARTS! of the Hungarian and Polish nations! men whose ALLIANCE would have SECURED THE SUCCOUR of THOUSANDS and TENS OF THOUSANDS of those yet valiant and mighty, though enslaved people! A Council of War numbering two such men, would have marked the ERA of the future FREEDOM of the WORLD! **Without the aid** of such men, the **Governments** of Western Europe must **sink** deeper and **deeper** in the **quagmire** into which they have **dragged themselves!** What has been the result of the Western Governments **neglecting** to declare on the side of Poland and Hungary? Why, the Polish arms that have been **turned against them** in the **bloody** and **obstinate** encounters in the Crimea would, on the Polish frontiers, have been REVERSED! accompanied with friendly and enthusiastic acclamations! hailing with shouts of true Patriotism, their ALLIES and DELIVERERS!

Another **fatality** is apparent by reason of the **Crimean Expedition,** when we consider that it gave **Russia time** and **opportunity** to fortify Poland, in raising impregnable barriers to an invading army, and investing that country with an array of troops that few nations, if any, had ever the misfortune to groan under. However, the **worst** and **most diabolical** feature of the case manifests itself in the **Russian barbarity!** that ensued under such military occupation, when the peaceful inhabitants were treated **without Mercy!** and in the most **revolting and cruel** manner, that the very **Fiends of Hell** could not equal! I will here give in a note one out of a number of such cases, the reading of which makes the blood *thrill through my veins!* I wish I could spare my readers the infliction of perusing such an account ; but as it is the TRUTH, and when we consider what the sufferings of those whom we ought so *dearly to remember and love* had to endure, let us SHARE WITH THEM THEIR GRIEFS and join in the **general lamentation,** by *shedding the burning heartfelt tears of Patriotism* for the sufferers of unhappy Poland!—for the sufferings of Paternal and Maternal **woe!** (1)

There is another account, of a still more recent date, which I feel it my duty to lay before the reader, as speaking trumpet-tongued against the **fatal Crimean Expedition!** which, among other alarming features, exhibits the levy by Russia of more than **60,000 Polish Troops within the last year!** and who would now be on the side of the Allies if they had but taken a step in the right direction. (2)

---

(1) A Letter from Cracow, dated Tuesday, the 2d of January, 1855, and appearing in the *Constitutionnel*, says:—
"The recruiting among the Jews, and the **carrying off** for the Military Schools of Jewish **Children** aged from **eight to ten!** causes amongst that class of inhabitants in Poland **indescribable terror and desolation!** In all the Towns and Villages near Kielce nothing but **weeping and lamentation is to be heard! Mothers tear their hair and beat their heads against the walls ! ! !** and Fathers sacrifice their **last penny!** to buy off their **Sons!**
"Recently an unfortunate man, whose **Eldest Son,** though just about to be married, had been **carried off,** went to the chief town of the province to beg that a younger son, who accompanied him, might be taken instead of his brother, but the **Second Son** was likewise **taken,** and the **Elder was not given up!** This gave such a **shock** to the Father that he was **taken ill,** and in **three days** died ! !
"The **manner** in which unfortunate **recruits** are **treated is** really cruel ! Thus, for example, those assembled at Kielce were not long since, **in spite of the cold, placed quite naked in rows in the street to undergo medical inspection ! !** "
(2) "Cracow, Tuesday, January 9, 1855.—The accounts received from the other side of the frontier continue to give a **melancholy** picture of the state of things in **Russian Poland,** and the greater part of the **weight of the war** appears to be thrown—and perhaps not **undesignedly**—on the shoulders of that **unfortunate Country!** Measures are being taken for **hermetically closing the long line of frontier towards Germany,** and cutting off all communication. At present the frontier guards allow travellers to pass into Poland, provided their passports are *en règle,* and their names are not to be found in the **List of the Proscribed;** but it is very difficult to get out again, so that comparatively but few persons take advantage of the permission, and those only on business of the last importance. **Overwhelming as are the forced contributions of provisions for the troops and provender for the horses which the Inhabitants of Poland have to make** as their quota of the **war expenses,** they may be considered light in comparison with those to which the Provinces of Podolia and the Ukraine are subjected. Those of Podolia alone amounted to SEVERAL MILLIONS OF SILVER ROUBLES during the past year; and these **forced contributions will never be paid for!** Several thousand waggons, which, with the necessary number of horses and drivers, were required by the Government in the month of

f 2

Another account, of a later date, informs us that **20,000 Poles** were seized and **dragged away** at **the dead hour of midnight!** from their fathers, wives, and children, by orders of the **Hell-Fiend Russian Despot!**

My Brother Patriots, let us now come to the plain question of WHAT IS TO BE DONE, AND HOW ARE WE TO DO IT? There can be no doubt on our minds as to the **enfeebled state of internal Poland,** more especially within the **last year!** and that that nation could not, *single*-handed, expel her oppressors. If Poland is to rise again into life! it will be from the sympathy and succour derived from the NATIONAL RESOURCES of Western Europe. I would put one question to you by way of parenthesis :—Is there any prospect of that desired advent taking place under the **Government alliance** as at present existing between Great Britain and France? I will take for granted that your reply will be in the negative. If so, what is to be done? Are we to allow our NATIONAL SYMPATHY to be sacrificed through a **want** of that **representative sympathy** on the part of the Government? Again, I take it for granted that your response will be "*No!*" Well, WHAT is to be DONE, and HOW are we TO DO IT? that is the interrogatory. First of all, as a Nation, we must KNOW and FEEL our own INDEPENDENCE. If we look in **false dependence** on a **Government** that **disregards** our NATIONAL APPEALS we become worse than **slaves,** and our **supposed Freedom a mockery** and a **delusion!**

In reference to various Meetings that have been held of late in England on behalf of Poland, I would wish to say a little. Although I have never personally attended any of those meetings,

---

September last, for the transport of provisions, baggage, and soldiers, have not only not yet been returned, but have actually **never since been heard of!** They may have been **sent to Siberia,** or be sticking at this moment in the **impassable sloughs of the Crimea!**

"In many of the frontier towns of Podolia,— for instance, at Kaminitz,— hundreds of waggons are kept in readiness to be loaded at **a moment's notice with the Public Treasury, Archives, and Books, and** carry them to a place of **safety** more inland. These waggons are relieved every fortnight.

"**Recruiting is carried on** in Poland to a greater extent, and with more oppressive severity, than in Russia Proper. The third levy in particular was most heavily felt, so that when it is completed, Poland will have but few men left capable of bearing arms. More than 60,000 men have been raised in Poland during the past year"!!!

still I have been a silent observer of the Patriotic feeling of the Nation exhibited on such occasions; and it has been a source of grief to me that they were unattended with any practical results. Resolutions were proposed and seconded in eloquent appeals; numerous Petitions to Parliament received the enthusiastic approval of crowded assemblies; and in the usual formality the Petitions were presented to the House of Commons, and ordered (as a matter of course) to "*lie on the table*" ! But when the all-important subject of those Petitions came to be considered and discussed, the NATIONAL FEELING of Great Britain was **trampled upon,** and suffered to die a natural death in the hands of a **traitorous Government!** Should that be so, my Brothers? Are the feelings of a nation to be ignored after such a fashion? But let me see, I fancy I discover a **want** of a GENERAL NATIONAL SYMPATHY that requires to be AROUSED! Those Meetings, although numerous, were **not general.** I fear we cannot term them general expressions of Patriotism, from which the BODY of the Nation, taken as a whole, stood **isolated!** The former exhibition of Patriotism that emanated previous to and at the time Poland was Partitioned, proved unsuccessful from a similar cause. A **limited** movement seldom makes an impression; whereas, a GENERAL and CONTINUOUS MOVEMENT, on the contrary, is sure to carry its weight. However, I would not wish it to be supposed that it is my object (in the present critical state of the world) to have a general feeling of Patriotism aroused for no other purpose than to **waste** the precious moments in the **idle and dangerous** folly of preparing "**Petitions for Parliament**"! and sending "**Addresses**"! to the Queen. If such were to be the upshot of the **national feeling!** I say **down with it for ever!** There is no greater **Bugbear** to the rational and meditative mind when it beholds that **unreflecting mania** which has taken possession of the **obscured comprehensions** of not a few, who are vainly hoping and endeavouring to accomplish some **good** through that **apparently** most **prolific** yet **sadly delusive** source, the **House of Commons!**

In answer to the question, what is to be done for the relief of Poland and Hungary, and how are we to set about it? I will here give my views in a condensed form, on this MOST IMPORTANT of all earthly considerations! Would that I could give the whole of my sentiments and convictions on this momentous subject; but it will altogether depend upon how my Abstract views are responded to, when, if successful in arousing the **dormant spirit** of Patriotism, it will afford me (D.V.) considerable gratification in coming forward and giving the whole of my plans in a subsequent publication.

As a preliminary observation, I have to call the attention of my Brother Patriots to the second PROPHETIC VISION! in the Drama of "THE FALL OF POLAND," page 70, which foretells that Poland will be RAISED UP from her low and prostrate condition by the intervention and through the instrumentality of "BRITANNIA," "GALLIA," "HIBERNIA," and "SCOTIA." However, in case there may be some in whose minds a doubt may arise as to the meaning I intend to convey, when they would **confound a Government** with a **National Agency!** I feel it my duty to remove that doubt, by drawing a wide distinction or line of demarcation between the two, and conferring the premeditated honour of rescuing Poland on the ALL-PREVAILING WILL OF THE NATION! In considering this all-important feature of the case, we must sever the **Anti-sympathetic will of the Government!** from the TRULY SYMPATHETIC WILL OF THE NATION; if we mingle the two together, the sympathetic is **lost!** in the **pernicious and preponderating** influence of the anti-sympathetic!

As the Polish and Hungarian Nations are precluded by the **tyrannic will** of **despots** from holding a Legislative Assembly, Diet, or Confederation, in their own countries, may I ask, will the NATIONAL WILL AND FREEDOM of this country preclude our Brothers in exile from holding such councils in Great Britain? I very much mistake the character and sympathetic feeling of this Nation for those oppressed countries, if any opposition would be raised against such a desired object. Well, to come to the point and give you the Abstract :—

First of all, we must learn to KNOW OURSELVES INDIVIDUALLY, as so many UNITS of which the British Nation as a WHOLE should be composed and made up. When we have an individual knowledge of ourselves, we will aspire to the knowledge of those around us, by which the happy effect is produced of feeling that we know and are known by the kindred sympathies of ourselves and others, forming one delightful harmony, when as a Nation we will become an UNDIVIDED BODY!

At present, I regret to say that the British Nation is composed of a vast number of **disjointed parts**! which we must *knit* together, before we can have any prospect of stirring and moving the National Machine in the right direction.

Religious **bigotry**! divides many; Tory, Whig, Radical, and Conservative principles, &c., divide others; and a vast conglomeration of parties and sects, all striving (with a contemptible vanity!) one against another, serve to destroy the symmetrical form of our National greatness!

The **evil eye** of **Governments** well know and **encourage** such **disorders;** when they are enabled to take a **treacherous advantage** of the **national imbecility** that presents itself, and **ride rough shod** over the flickering spirit of Patriotism, which now and then emanates from the HEART of the NATION!

Oh! my Fellow-Men, I implore of you,—I entreat of you,—I beseech of you, in the name of the Great and All-powerful God, who presides over the destinies of all nations, and for the sake of his Son Our Crucified Redeemer, give up this **awful discord,** and join in the soul and spirit of true Patriotism, which knows and feels no other sentiment than that of love to God and love to one another. If we are **not a nation in unity** with ourselves, how can we call upon the French Nation to JOIN us in our exertions for the regeneration of Poland and Hungary?

I will now draw to a conclusion, by giving a brief outline of what I propose to be the Rules for the Formation of a National Constitution.

RULES

FOR THE FORMATION

OF A

NATIONAL CONSTITUTION

THROUGHOUT

Britannia, Gallia, Hibernia, and Scotia;

HAVING FOR ITS OBJECT

THE RESTORATION OF POLAND AND HUNGARY,

AND

THE PROTECTION OF GREAT BRITAIN AND FRANCE,

FROM THE PREMEDITATED

INVASION AND CONQUEST OF ALL EUROPE

AND ITS ADJACENT ISLANDS

By the RUSSIAN DESPOT.

~~~~~~~~~~~~~~~~~

RULE I.

In order to put down the **aggressive system** Russia has pursued and so **obstinately** carried on during and since the time of Peter the " Great," it is absolutely necessary, as a SAFE-GUARD to Europe, Asia, and the World, to ARREST the **pre-meditated invasion !** of France and the British Islands by

RE-ESTABLISHING the NATIONALITY OF POLAND and HUNGARY, the ONLY CHANNEL through which **that aggression** can be OVER-COME! and the "Balance of Power" in Europe restored and upheld.

RULE II.

To effect the RESTORATION of Poland and Hungary, a SELF-NATIONAL UNION, APART from any **Government connection,** must be formed in each of the Four Western European Countries, bearing the respective denominations : — Britannia, Gallia, Hibernia, and Scotia.

RULE III.

When the Four distinct SELF-NATIONAL UNIONS take place, having in view the one great and SELF-SAME OBJECT, the **present diseased national** state will be REMOVED, and a PRO-PHYLACTIC against any *future disorders* infused, by reason of a vast Quadruple Alliance in the NATIONAL SUPPORTING UNION of the Four Countries.

RULE IV.

In order to obtain an INDIVIDUAL NATIONAL UNION in each country, there must be encouraged and created in each an individual and CONTINUOUS NATIONAL MOVEMENT.

RULE V.

In order to effect an Individual National Movement, a *primary* appeal will be necessary TO AROUSE THE SYMPATHIES AND PATRIOTISM OF ALL! through the instrumentality of a General Agency.

RULE VI.

For the purpose of establishing a GENERAL AGENCY, it will be necessary to hold a PRELIMINARY MEETING in London ; comprising the most prominent and ACTIVE PATRIOTS, numbering Poles, Hungarians, French, English, Irish, and Scotch.

RULE VII.

Let said Meeting form a PROVISIONAL COMMITTEE, which subsequently is to be consolidated into a PERMANENT COMMITTEE, with permission to add to the numerical PATRIOTISM of said Committee as the GREAT NATIONAL CAUSE ADVANCES.

RULE VIII.

Among the Proceedings and Plans that said Committee may devise in the regulation of a general Agency, let them adopt one in particular, viz. prepare a Notice to the effect that " A GRAND NATIONAL DEMONSTRATION will be held on a given day, in support of the cause of Poland and Hungary! and for the protection of Western Europe from a **premeditated Invasion by Russia**"! &c. &c. Let said Notice be printed and published in *four* forms :—1st, As Placards, to be exhibited in the public thoroughfares throughout every city, town, and village, in the aforesaid countries, printing a certain number in the French language for posting throughout France. 2nd, As conspicuous Advertisements in the public journals, set out in a LARGER TYPE than is generally adopted, with signs of exclamation! and so forth, to *arrest the attention* of those who seldom read Advertisements. 3rd, To have struck off from 100,000 to 200,000 copies, or more, as the case may be, of said Notice in the form of Hand Bills, to be distributed throughout the LENGTH and BREADTH of the aforesaid countries. 4th, Have struck off the required number of Letters embodying said Notice, with some alterations giving it an epistolary character, and have them duly directed and forwarded through the General Post Office to the *principal* and *leading men* throughout what is now **erroneously termed** the " **United Kingdom** of Great Britain and Ireland," as also that of France, calling on said influential Gentlemen for their attendance and support at the aforesaid GRAND NATIONAL DEMONSTRATION and if there are any of those to whom said Notices are sent who do not feel disposed or willing to respond thereto, it will be the duty of the Secretary of the National Committee *to forestall* such indisposition by appending at the foot of each Letter, in Postscript-form, a request that such Gentleman or Gentlemen will be pleased to notify same in writing, together with his or their **reasons** for **not joining** the GRAND NATIONAL DEMONSTRATION. And, furthermore, let said **reasons** or **objections,** if any, be *Enrolled* and *Registered* in a Book or Books kept for that purpose, the Secretary taking the precaution to file all the original documents, with the envelopes of same annexed to each, in order to preserve the *post-mark*, in case said documents may subsequently have to be referred to, as occasion may offer and the members of the National Constitution may think proper. And, furthermore, in the event of any case or cases arising where **No Notice!** is taken of said Letters, it will be the duty of the Secretary, after the lapse of fourteen or twenty-one days at farthest, to note down opposite the **Name!** of each party the words "**No Answer!**" to be afterwards made use of as the Members of the National Constitution may *deem fit.*

RULE IX.

Taking it for granted that said National Demonstration is convened and successful by a full attendance on the part of the several deputations from the aforesaid countries, it is then the duty of the Meeting to PROCEED TO WORK, and to SELECT and APPOINT from among the ASSEMBLED DEPUTATIONS FOUR COMMITTEES, to be denominated the " Central Permanent National Committees," in manner following :—1st, The English National Committee, already formed into a Provisional to become a Central Permanent National Committee for all England. 2nd, A French Central Permanent National Committee for all France. 3rd, An Irish Central Permanent National Committee for all Ireland. 4th, A Scotch Central Permanent National Committee for all Scotland.

RULE X.

The aforesaid Central Committees are to hold WEEKLY or more frequent MEETINGS, as the case may demand, in PUBLIC EDIFICES,

g

selected and appropriated for that purpose ONLY, in the Metropolitan Towns of London, Paris, Dublin, and Edinburgh.

RULE XI.

In order to SPREAD THE PATRIOTIC movement, and to make it become GENERAL and LASTING, it will be the duty of the several Central Committees to form BRANCH ASSOCIATIONS, by which the Arterial System of the Sympathetic Patriotism of the Country may be kept up in UNISON with the Main or Central Artery, flowing on in UNINTERRUPTED healthful action, imparting LIFE and ANIMATION to each member of the National body.

RULE XII.

Independent of the Weekly Meetings to be held by the Four Central Committees in their respective localities, it will be necessary to convene a MONTHLY MEETING in London, comprising the English Central Committee, with deputations from the French, Irish, and Scotch Central Committees, for the purpose of ascertaining the General feeling, and how far the National Cause has progressed, and to consult upon what means may be further devised for the National development taken COLLECTIVELY.

RULE XIII.

Out of the materials composed of the COMBINED NATIONAL WILL of the Western Sons of Liberty may be laid the foundation and erected that Glorious Structure—a NATIONAL CONSTITUTION! which is to GUIDE the NATIONAL WILL on the PATH to VICTORY **against Russian aggression and Despotism!** (1)

---

(1) Of the Laws by which the National Constitution will be regulated I dispense with the task (from their voluminous import) of giving even an abstract recital; but show in the subsequent Rules the main object the National Constitution will have at heart.

RULE XIV.

In a FINANCIAL point of view, the National Constitution will be AMPLY PROVIDED for, in the PATRIOTIC ENDEAVOURS of EACH INDIVIDUAL MEMBER, without having to place themselves under the **humiliating posture** as **mendicants** before the **closed portals** of the **Government Treasury !**

RULE XV.

A CORRESPONDING AGENCY is constantly to be kept up between the Members of the National Constitution and the Polish and Hungarian nations, who are to be informed of the glorious work in progress for obtaining their National Freedom.

RULE XVI.

Polish Soldiers who are forced to serve in the ranks of the Russian Despot are also to be communicated with, and informed of the period when they may reckon on their *deliverance*, when the *crushed spirit of patriotism* will *rise once more* in their breasts, and BURST the **bonds of the oppressor** in a successful revolt!

RULE XVII.

The PRIMARY object the National Constitution will have in view is to RAISE a certain number of TROOPS throughout Britannia, Gallia, Hibernia, and Scotia, for the purpose of acting against the Russian, Prussian, and Austrian forces.

RULE XVIII.

The number of Troops to be levied must amount to 500,000, of which 300,000 will be kept on active service, the other 200,000 forming a recruiting reserve in case of casualties.

RULE XIX.

After said body of men (300,000) go through the regular Military discipline, under the orders of proper Officers in the British and French Service, assisted by skilful Polish and Hungarian Generals, they are to proceed, with all their artillery and battering-rams, through Germany, PUTTING DOWN **all opposition !** that may be raised by the Germanic Rus- Prus- and Austrian Tribes ; then ENTER POLAND), attack and seize all the fortresses, &c. (**recently erected**) at the SAME TIME ! taking the *precaution,* however (after securing the most **Prominent Ringleaders !** and expelling the remnant of the **Muscovite Barbarians !**), to HOLD said FORTRESSES and OCCUPY SAME with Troops, when the National Patriotism of the released and grateful Inhabitants will raise a NEW AND PERMANENT CONSTITUTION for the LASTING FREEDOM of POLAND, on the CZARTORYSKI DYNASTY !

RULE XX.

The erection of the New Polish Constitution is to be followed by SIMILAR VICTORIES **over the Austrian Troops** and the OCCUPATION OF HUNGARY, when the National Patriotism of the released and grateful inhabitants will raise a NEW AND PERMANENT CONSTITUTION for the LASTING FREEDOM of HUNGARY, on the KOSSUTH DYNASTY !

RULE XXI.

When the RECONSTRUCTION of POLAND and HUNGARY takes place, THEN, and NOT TILL THEN ! will the PEACE OF EUROPE and the WORLD be RESTORED, and the TRUE BALANCE OF POWER ESTA-BLISHED and MAINTAINED !

One parting word, and I have done.

As a medium in the hands of the public, the Drama of "THE

FALL OF POLAND" may be made an instrument for arousing the **dormant** Patriotism and Sympathy of Western Europe on behalf of unhappy Poland, whether as an HISTORICAL production, to be read to the assembled family around the domestic hearth, or as the property of the general public, who would feel desirous of seeing the Drama brought forward on the Stage.

I am one of those who consider that the Stage has its USE as well as its **abuse** :—its USE comes in question when an instructive Historical *reality* is pourtrayed ; its **abuse !** when **Fiction** is put forward as an **alleged historical fact !**

Of all historical facts, I am persuaded there is none nearer to the HEART ! of true Patriotism than the unhappy fate of Poland in 1794, when the NOBLE KOSCIUSKO FELL, pierced and covered with wounds, in DEFENCE OF THE GLORIOUS CAUSE OF FREEDOM ! and to which historical fact, together with the historical circumstances that led thereto, the Drama strictly adheres, and faithfully represents.

I have no doubt, that if the Drama of " THE FALL OF POLAND" could be EFFICIENTLY brought forward on the Stage at the PRESENT TIME, when the public mind is looking on all sides with the most intense anxiety to see " WHEN ?" and " HOW ?" Poland will be " RIGHTED," that it would go far to establish a BEGINNING to the "GRAND NATIONAL DEMONSTRATION" and "NATIONAL CONSTITUTION" I have already referred to, as the MEANS BY and THROUGH which Poland will be raised up, from her low and prostrate state,—

> " To the bright pinnacle of Liberty,—
> An Ornament to Nations; bless'd on Earth,
> While water'd with the dews from Heav'n above."

With feelings of the most devoted attachment to the Glorious and Immortal Cause of Patriotism, I beg leave again to subscribe myself, the faithful Brother of all True Friends and Promoters of Liberty,

A PATRIOT.

3d of May (1), 1855.

---

(1) The Sixty-fourth Anniversary of the NEW CONSTITUTION, 3d of May, 1791, when Poland for a time had breathed the air of Freedom !

ERRATA OF REMARKS.

Page xxxvii. lines 28 and 29, *for* " and to establish, as formerly, an independent kingdom under the ancient and illustrious house of Hapsburg," *read* " and to establish a free and independent Constitutional Government." The reason the Author was led into this inadvertent mistake, arose from the *Historical Fact*, that the first Prince of the House of Hapsburg who reigned in Hungary (Ferdinand I.) was elected King of Hungary by the *unanimous consent* of the *Hungarian Diet* in 1526. (1)

Page xxxix. lines 2 and 3, *for* " 17th of March," *read* " 17th of February."

Page xlv. line 3, *for* " is that of the Germanic States," *read* " are those of the Germanic States."

Page lv. lines 5 and 6, *for* " that there **never was a falser statement!** from the lips of any Minister!" *read* " that there **never fell from the lips of any Minister a falser statement!**"

Page lix. line 28, *for* " Russian intermeddling," *read* " Prussian intermeddling."

---

(1) Hapsburg, or Habsburg, is a village of Switzerland, with ruins of a castle, the original seat of the present imperial family of Austria, from whence originated the denomination of the " House of Hapsburg."

THE

FALL OF POLAND.

THE POLISH ARMS.

POLAND (*King of*). QUARTERLY: *first* and *fourth*, gu. (1), an EAGLE displayed ar. (2) beaked, membered, and CROWNED or (3) for Poland: *second* and *third*, gules, a CAVALIER, completely accoutred in Armour, on a Horse in full speed, argent, in his dexter (4) hand a drawn sword; on the sinister (5), a shield azure (6), thereon a Patriarchal Cross argent for Lithuania (Jagellon): over all an Escutcheon of *Pretence*, per fesse sable (7) and argent (8): two swords in saltier (9), their points in chief gules, hilts (10), and pommels (11), or impaling (12) Saxony.

THE POLISH CREST.

POLAND (*King of*). On an Imperial CROWN an EAGLE displayed, as in the ARMS; the shield encompassed with the Ensigns of the Order of the WHITE EAGLE.

THE POLISH COCKADE.

The Polish Cockade is composed of Azure representing the *Sapphire* and Planet *Jupiter*; the Or or Amaranth, representing the *Topaz* and Planet *Sol.* The *outer* circle of the Cockade is formed by the BLUE RIBBON; the *inner* circle, centre, and body thereof are formed by the YELLOW or GOLD RIBBON. The Cockade Colours of Poland, in preference to others, have been adopted as the most NATIONAL and suitable for the Cover of this Book :—1st, the Blue cloth; 2nd, the Arms and Crest of Poland stamped thereon in Gold or Amaranth (13).

THE HUNGARIAN COCKADE.

The Hungarian Cockade is composed of Gules representing the *Ruby* and Planet *Mars;* the Argent representing the *Pearl* and Planet *Luna;* the Vert representing the *Emerald* and Planet *Venus.* The *outer* circle of the Cockade is formed by the RED RIBBON; the next circle thereto is formed by the WHITE RIBBON; and the inner circle, centre, and body thereof are formed by the GREEN RIBBON.

Annotations explanatory of the coloured Arms, &c. of Poland.

(1) Gu. or Gules, red. (2) Ar. or Argent, white or silver. (3) Or, yellow or gold. (4) Dexter, right. (5) Sinister, left. (6) Azure, blue. (7) Escutcheon, semi-black. (8) Escutcheon, semi-white. (9) Saltier, in the form of a cross. (10) Hilts, handles. (11) Pommels, the knots that balance the blades of the swords. (12) Impaling, halving or dividing. (13) The reason why the term Amaranth is used by the Poles as expressive of one of their National Colours, takes its rise from the Swedish Order of Knighthood, termed the Amaranta or Amaranth, representing a Jewel of Gold, and which colour forms the body and centre of the Polish Cockade. This Order was instituted in the year 1645, by Christina, Queen of Sweden, daughter of Gustavus Adolphus, in honour of a lady of the name of Amaranta, equally celebrated for beauty and virtue; but the Order did not survive the foundress. The ensign of the Order was a JEWEL OF GOLD, composed of two great A's joined together, one being reversed, enriched on both sides with diamonds, and set within a wreath of laurel leaves, headed with white, bearing the motto " Dolce nella memoria." This badge was worn either pendent to a gold chain or a crimson or blue ribbon at pleasure. Amaranth is also a botanical term; and used in poetry as denoting an imaginary unfading flower.

AN
HISTORICAL TRAGIC DRAMA
OF THE FALL OF

POLAND.
1794.

DRAMATIS PERSONÆ.

POLES—MEN.

Kosciusko .... *the Polish Dictator and Generalissimo.*
Madalinski .... *a friend, General, and Ambassador thereof.*
Dzialinski .... *Do. Do. and husband of Chrysillida.*
Kollontay .... *Do. Do. and consort of Radziwilla.*
Prince Charles, *a Mute, about* 15 *years of age (appearing only in Act* II. *Scene* 1, *and Act* IV. *Scene* 6), *a Lithuanian, and son of the Princess Lubomirski.*

PRUSSIANS—MEN.

Frederic William .... *the King of Prussia.*
Bucholz .... *his Minister of State and Ambassador.*

RUSSIANS—MEN.

Sievers .... *a Minister of State.*
Igolstrum .... *Do. his successor.*
Suwarrow. .... *General.*
Ferzen .... *General.*

FEMALE RUSSIANS.

Catherine II. .... *the Empress of Muscovy or all the Russias.*
Her Maids of Honor, *Mute (appearing only in Act* III. *Sc.* 3).

FEMALE POLES.

Princess Lubomirski, *a Lithuanian, and mother to Prince Charles.*
Chrysillida .... *the spouse of Dzialinski.*
Radziwilla .... *the consort of Kollontay.*

Polish, Prussian, and Russian Soldiers, etc.

DRAMATIS PERSONÆ

OF

THE RESPECTIVE SCENES.

THE DRAMA.

FALL OF POLAND.

ACT I. SCENE I.

A Hall, in an ancient castle, with central pillars.

Enter BUCHOLZ and SIEVERS, in converse with each other.

BUCH. I almost pity that deluded King.

SIEV. Pity! I almost hold him in disdain.
Couldst thou suppose that he, who now delights
In all the follies of this wild uproar,—
Hath giv'n this very Constitution up,
This new concocted scheme of liberty?

BUCH. Indeed!

SIEV. It is a bubble that will shortly burst,
An evanescent mania of th' times.
No later than last night he fully spoke
Th' various workings of his feeble mind;
Told me he'd play the fool to-day, and strive
With all his might to wipe the sin away
By penance and contrition on th' morrow.

BUCH. Then I'd pronounce him—but it matters not;
The proper comment in your *thoughts* supply.

B

Is he not head of that confed'rate clan
Who first dissented from his love of change?

SIEV. You mean the Council of Targowica?

BUCH. The very same.

SIEV. Odd as it seems, he's now their President,
Thus heading his opponents 'gainst himself.

BUCH. Whence did that strange anomaly arise?

SIEV. The Empress with her own consummate skill
Compell'd the wayward King to undulate
In retrospective course, like Ocean's tide.
Nor could the sea surpass him in that point,
So regularly he both ebbs and flows
Within the space that measures day and night.

BUCH. That Council, too, forgetful whence it sprang,
Of late appears to roll from side to side.

SIEV. *There* is the greater marvel! what a scene!
The Polish Sov'reign first to them consigns
His love of liberty :—and they, in turn,
Most shamefully desert th' Imperial cause,
T' burn their incense at the shrine of Freedom.

BUCH. (*looking to one side.*)
Behold! the Polish chieftain is at hand;—
He comes with Kollontay;—let us retire,
With open *ears*, if not with open *arms*,
To wait his salutation;—whispers oft
Whole volumes of intelligence impart.
(*They cautiously withdraw towards the rear.*)

Enter (*in front*) KOSCIUSKO *and* KOLLONTAY.

KOS. Is it the King they seek?

KOL. No, but thyself, O Chief;—in haste they glide
Like birds of rapine on the stormy wind.

Kos.   Then let them come, like vultures to the gale
      Of human carnage, and select their prey.

Kol.   I trust the victims will be our's to choose.

      (*Aside to Kosciusko, on perceiving the Envoys.*)
      But they are list'ning, and expect to gain
      The recompense of list'ners.

Kos.   The ear of Dionysius is long-fam'd;
      Perhaps his envoys gave it all its pow'r.

Kol.   Of this be certain,—these ambassadors
      Would form the *largest ear* in Christendom.

Kos.   Nothing more likely; yet, to waive that point,
      Are the troops ready for th' intended march?

Kol.   They are, rever'd Dictator.

Kos.   Haste, then,—return to thine expectant friends;
      Salute them all for me! nor fail to fly
      From that dark glen; th' moment you can do so,
      Leave it without delay,—I know it well.

  (*Aside, to himself.*)   (*Exit Kollontay.*)
      Thus have I ventur'd to resume the helm
      Amid the boiling surge of civil war.
      No other course was left me, save to sink
      Together with my country,—or with *her*
      To brave the scowling tempest that now reigns.
      At such a time th' office of Dictator
      Need not excite much envy, altho' arm'd
      With all the powers of supreme command.

      (*Turning round, and addressing the Ambassa-
      dors, who now come forward.*)
      Envoy of Russia, hail! and thou of Prussia!
      By what impell'd could two such potentates
      Yield such an honour with combin'd effect?

Siev.   (*somewhat embarrassed, and presenting a Letter.*)
      This letter from his Polish Majesty
      Will speak at once th' purport of our visit.

Kos. (*taking the Letter, and putting it in his pocket.*)
    Perhaps I need not read it, as inform'd
    Already, I anticipate its aim.

BOTH THE ENVOYS.
    Inform'd already!

Kos.   It takes away my military post,
    Leaving you free to cultivate your schemes,
    To put your wise, sagacious heads together,
    Planning a new dismemberment of Poland.

SIEV.   It is most strange!

BUCH.   I thought no Pole, save Stanislas himself,
    Could have an intimation of the kind.

SIEV.   Yet hold; perhaps this insight from thyself
    Alone takes rise in reason's deep discernment?

Kos.   No, truly, but from knowledge well deriv'd.

SIEV. (*sternly looking at Bucholz.*)
    Then, by the Just! there's one of us, past doubt,
    A faithless representative of royalty.

BUCH. (*retorting frown for frown.*)
    Nothing more true! and thou'rt the very man.

SIEV.   I cannot bear this imputation;—draw!

BUCH.   Thou'lt ever *find* me ready as thyself
    To vindicate mine honour; so come on!
        (*Both the Envoys unsheath their swords, and
        are about to engage each other.*)

Kos. (*interposing.*)
    Pause for awhile, rash men; attend to me.
    You neither told me, Sievers; nor did *you*,
    Bucholz:—and yet the meditated plot
    Hath reach'd mine ears from an undoubted source.
    Of this no more. My author I'll reveal
    Never,—long as the current of my life
    Pursues her earthly course. Thus you shall know
    How well I keep *my* secrets; while your thoughts,

Committed to the vagrancy of speech,
Can waft their way with circulating pow'r.
Put up your swords, then, with prudential valour,
And use them only in your country's cause.
I blame not those who're faithful to their trust,
Whate'er their climate or their nation be.

> (*The Envoys sheath their swords.*)

SIEV. Most gen'rous chieftain, with such noble views,
I think your int'rest at the Russian court
Might yet be of vast moment, and, no doubt,
The harbinger of blessings to this land.
The Empress only needs to know you well,
To take you to her counsels and esteem.

(*Drawing Kosciusko aside.*)

Weary of others and their veering course,
Suppose she ev'n conferr'd on thee a sceptre ;
Would Kosciusko deign to cultivate
Imperial friendship for an *honour'd* crown ?

KOS. What ! dost thou dare t' play upon *mine* honour,
Perturbate spirit of the Northern blast ?—
To blunt my energies, or cool them down
To the low standard of your freezing point ?
May Hell herself, with all her seas of fire,
First light upon my soul; or whirl me up,
Amid her rarer elements of wrath,
The awful sport of her electric flames !
Or may the Universe in one vast orb
Of desolating rage, roll wave on wave,
And thunder at my lot with ceaseless ire,—
Ere I forget my country, or become
The frigid creature of a *Despot's smiles !*
No ;—'tis revolting to my inmost pore ;—
Far other objects animate my mind ;—
The renovation of my native land,—

The restoration of her plunder'd rights,—
Th' re-establishment of all her glory ;—
These, these alone, can plant their standard *there,*
Or gain an endless empire in my heart.
        (*The Envoys seem struck with astonishment ;
        and Kosciusko wheels round.*)
    (*taking out the Letter, and opening it.*)
        Now for the royal favour;

                            Let me read.
            (*He silently peruses it. Sievers keeps pacing
            about in deep thought ; meanwhile*)
BUCH. (*aside.*)
        What could the Russian minister have said
        To draw forth such a torrent of disdain ?
        A certain species of concealment hangs
        O'er all his projects; and, though join'd with me
        Ostensibly in this momentous bus'ness,
        He never falters at abstruse designs.
        How fortunate it is that he's recall'd,
        And only waits for Igolstrum's arrival !
        Ev'n in the interim, however short,
        His dubious counsels I'll no longer brook ;—
        No ;—to the Empress let me now repair,
        And there consult my royal sire, her guest.
        No doubt, this herald, when he finds me gone,
        Will follow me as swiftly as the wind ;—
        To try him, then, on bottom,—off I go.
    (*Contumeliously, and still aside.*)
        Poor superseded Sievers! fare thee well !
                            (*Exit Bucholz.*)
KOS. (*aside, ceasing to read.*)
        I now begin to penetrate their object :
        Dismiss'd by Stanislas, these wise men say,
        Let us detach him from the pop'lar cause.

'Tis deeply plann'd, and worthy of its source.
(*To Sievers.*)
How soon do you expect to see the King?

SIEV. Perhaps to-day; and we, in truth, consented
To this mediation, solely because
'Tis confidential and requires despatch.

Kos. Then be it so,—and short be *my* reply.
Tell him his Gen'ral hath resign'd the trust
Held by the sanction of his Majesty;—
Nor fail to tell him that my country's chief,
The new Dictator, will protect him *still*.

SIEV. Excuse me, Kosciusko, but this seems
Far too indefinite or undefin'd.

Kos. Fear not, friend Sievers, he'll understand me
As thoroughly as you do; and I'm sure
I need not go beyond that ample test.
(*Exit Kosciusko.*)

SIEV. (*solus, looking all around.*)
But where is Bucholz? I must after him.
His flight on this occasion seems unkind.
(*Exit Sievers, in great haste.*)

(*The Scene changes.*)

ACT I. Scene II.

A garden, having two splendid vistas therein, one near one side, and the other near the opposite side. These vistas command a long perspective opening on a distant country. Halfway down the vistas you can go from one to the other by a cross avenue, which is altogether unseen by the audience.

———

Enter, near the front, Catherine and Frederic, in converse.

CATH. (*aside.*)
    I ne'er beheld so subtle an opponent;
    Just as you think he's captur'd, off he goes
    To rhapsodize the beauties of a flow'r.
FRED. Why is the Empress silent?
CATH. She pauses for his Majesty's reply.
FRED. We both are pausing then.
CATH. (*aside.*)
    His ingenuity exceeds belief;
    He sports away his adversary's lunge,
    And renders triumph pow'rless as defeat.
FRED. Is it Minerva's resolute intent
    To probe my motives with such keen desire?
CATH. (*aside.*)
    There is another parry, thus to turn
    My opposition into vain conceit.
FRED. Speak, mighty Empress, or my thoughts surmise
    The coming of Bellona in a storm.

CATH. (*aside.*)

    Minerva and Bellona! Wisdom, War!—
    What shall I next become?

FRED.   O that I knew the title best belov'd!
    I'd give it from the bottom of my heart,
    To tempt this angel into speech once more.

CATH. (*aside.*)

    I'll torture him with silence, till I gain
    The answer his duplicity withholds.
    He knows not Cath'rine, who *presumes* to play
    Upon her intellect, or dares to fly
    To such expedients on the gravest points.

FRED.   Fairest Diana, wilt thou ne'er respond?
    O that I had the memorable lyre
    Of long-fam'd Orpheus! I would make the woods,
    The floods, the very rocks reverberate
    T' awaken nature from her speechless trance.

CATH. (*aside.*)

    I cannot stand it longer. (*To him.*) Hear me, sir;
    The subject of our conference demands
    A plain and candid answer;—hence I swear
    T' speak with thee *no more*, till I obtain it.

    (*Hereupon, Catherine suddenly enters one of
    the vistas, and is immediately followed by
    Frederic in an apparently supplicating
    manner. They appear there in conversation
    for some time, till they pass into the cross
    avenue; meanwhile*)

Enter (in front) SIEVERS *and* FERZEN.

SIEV.   The cause of my dismissal is so strange,
    I'm half inclin'd to think the Empress will
    On due reflection change her hasty course.

FERZ.   It is not *easy* to revoke *her* acts.

SIEV.   Wilt thou assist me?

FERZ.   Yes, if I really can serve thy suit;—
But, should thy prospects, like a misty cloud,
Rest on no better basis than *mere air*,
You need not calculate on my support.

SIEV.   No, certainly; nor should I think t' engage
In any *fruitless* effort to regain
The royal favour;—*that* would make bad *worse*.

FERZ.   Perhaps 'twere better first to feel your way,
Relying on thy personal repute.
Let me reflect. The Empress is at hand;—
Suppose you seek an interview to-day?
Some op'ning might be gain'd. Yet do not press
Thine application beyond certain bounds.
If at the outset you receive repulse,
Retire immediately, and rest assur'd
All present hopes of victory are gone.

SIEV.   Such is my own impression. Hence, at first,
I'll try mine unassisted influence.
As an important matter leads thee, also,
To an interview, mark how rolls the tide,
Whether propitious or against thy friend.
If needful, and if likely to succeed,
Give him thine aid, and help him into port.
But, lo! th' invidious Bucholz now approaches,
And with him, Madalinski. Let's withdraw!

> (*They go merely a short distance from the
> front, into one of the vistas, so as to remain
> there in view to the audience. Meanwhile,
> Catherine and Frederic, having quitted the
> cross avenue, and thence entered (in that
> point) the other vista, and being for some
> time visible therein, now issue from it. Just
> as they come out of that vista*),

Enter MADALINSKI *and* BUCHOLZ, *meeting them there.*

CATH. (*coming forward.*)
    Count Oginski, what's your mission?
MADAL. (*aside.*)
    I'm taken for Oginski; 'tis as well.
(*To her*) Most mighty Empress, it of late appears
    Th' Polish Patriots have join'd in Council.
CATH. Hah!
MADAL. Their first decree to Kosciusko gives
    The office of Dictator!
CATH. The office of Dictator!
MADAL. E'en so; and they've another post conferr'd
    On their fam'd favourite, who now is chief
    In military influence and rank.
CATH. What have they done with your *illustrious* King?
MADAL. To use his Majesty's own words, they've eas'd
    The Monarch of a multitude of cares.
CATH. Yes! and 'tis well if he retain his crown.
MADAL. He prays an audience of th' great Tzarina,
    And hopes t'obtain it with monarchal grace.
CATH. Tell him he has it, and to come prepar'd.
      (*She looks around very significantly, and takes
       Madalinski aside, saying in a very angry
       whisper, as follows:*)
    Ay, let him come prepar'd, if possible,
    T' avert my resolution and disdain!
        (*Exit Madalinski, bowing.*)
FRED. (*to Bucholz.*)
    Bucholz, dost thou too, come t' amuse us all
    With like intelligence of Patriot Counsels?
      (*Bucholz takes a large official Letter out of his
       pocket, and presents it to King Frederic.*)

Buch. This letter will inform your Majesty.

> (*Frederic looks at the seal, and then at the direction.*)

Fred. How came you by it?

Buch. On an imprison'd courier it was found.

Fred. 'Tis not to me;—I cannot break the seal.
Go and despatch it to its destination.

Buch. What! ev'n to Kosciusko?

Fred. 'Tis to *him*.

Cath. What means this wayward playfulness, O King?
Permit me to peruse th' superscription.

Fred. Madam, receive it, with unbounded thanks
For the great honour thus conferr'd on me.

> (*Catherine takes the Letter from him, and reads aloud the direction thereof as follows:*)

> " To the Most Excellent
> "Thaddeus Kosciusko, &c. &c. &c.
> " Dictator and Generalissimo of Poland."

Cath. Fine titles for a *rebel!*

Fred. (*aside.*)
How harsh that epithet to such a man!

Cath. May I break the seal?

Fred. How could I sanction it?

Cath. Dost thou refuse me?

Fred. I leave th' Empress to her own *discretion.*

Cath. Discretion! What! with patriotic fools?

Fred. Do as you please, then, madam! I have done.

Cath. Then thus it pleaseth me.

> (*She dashes open the Letter with evident symptoms of great excitement, and proceeds to read its contents.*)

Fred. (*aside.*)
Oh! what an outrage! Shall I now retire,

And walk away with Bucholz by the arm?
'Twould serve th' lady as she justly merits;
But how should I accomplish my designs?
Ay, there's the rub! for Thorn and Dantzig both,
Those fam'd emporiums of commercial wealth,
Would thence be lost, and Prussia still depriv'd
Of that ascendancy for which I pant.
Down, then, my spirit, and prepare to kiss,
If requisite, her neat imperial foot.

BUCH. (*aside, to Frederic most gravely.*)
What hath your Majesty resolv'd to do?

FRED. (*humorously.*)
To kiss her, if she let me; that's *my* way.
Nor is't ignoble with her charming sex
T' abound in many sweet civilities.
Upon my honour, after all they say
Of Petticoat dominion, it oft serves
Our purpose *better*, and with *vast effect*.

BUCH. In matters of political intrigue,
It's sway is most illusive and severe.

FRED. That springs from gentlemen like thee, my friend,
Advising measures of a cêrtain class:—
But tell me, what would all the realms on earth,
And more especially their governments,
Do without lovely woman? Poh! 'tis plain,
If 'reft of that maternal source of being,
The world itself with all its peopled climes
Would soon become a den for beasts of prey.

BUCH. Thy arguments are too prolific, sire,
To be withstood on such a gen'ral base.
But in *this* instance e'en my *fancy fails*
T' expect an honour'd or approv'd result.

FRED. Be quiet, Bucholz; keep thy spirit down;
Be silent *in due season*, and behold ⚹

c

The happy *issue* with a Mentor's eye.
> (*Catherine comes forward, and takes Frederic aside.*)

CATH. Fred'ric, I wish to speak with thee in private.

FRED. I'm humbly at your service at all times.
> (*Catherine now perceives Sievers in waiting, and questions him sternly.*)

CATH. Sievers, your business?

SIEV. The seals of office have been ta'en away
From one who serv'd your Majesty most truly.

CATH. *There* we *differ.*

SIEV. Allow me to expostulate awhile!

CATH. No, not a word; my firm resolve is this,—·
Sievers, thou art my minister no more.
> (*She turns away from him, and recognises Ferzen. Exit Sievers.*)

Ferzen, what takes you here? I'm much surpris'd
You've left the seat of war. Is Polish pride
Sufficiently put down t' give you respite?

FERZ. Madam, I seek no respite; but I come
To do a kindness for an honour'd friend.
A Polish Count, who once preserv'd my life,
Is now in chains, and to Siberia goes—
Except Imperial mercy interfere.

CATH. Another time I'll hear thee on this point;
I'm not at leisure to decide it *now ;*—
Meanwhile, knock off his chains, and treat him well.
Go to the tented field without delay,
And there erase the spirit of revolt.

FERZ. I thank thee, mighty Empress, and obey.
> (*Exit Ferzen. Catherine takes Frederic aside, and there speaks as follows :*)

CATH. Fred'ric, you dine with me to-day. Invite
Your good ambassador at six o'clock.

Meanwhile, let him ramble where he pleases,
Or with some maid of honour play at chess.
This *patriot* mania dwells upon my mind,
And urges expedition on all sides.
Follow me, therefore, in convenient time;
Our counsels must be *secret* and *combin'd.*

(*Exit Catherine.*)

FRED.   Bucholz, what shall I give thee for thy thoughts?
BUCH.   Not much, indeed, O sire.   Your Majesty
Hath patience for a Stoic,—thus to brook
That admirable tyrant with such grace.
FRED.   Hold now, my grave philosopher, and learn
To speak with more decorum of thy host.
BUCH.   Host!
FRED.   Yes, you're to dine at her imperial table
This very day; and, in the interim,
With some fair maid of honour play at chess.
BUCH.   Really so!
FRED.   Grave as a Capuchin.
BUCH.   Then off I go—
FRED.   To play away till six o'clock.
BUCH.   Is that the festive hour, O King?
FRED.   It is; be punctual.   Yon vista leads thee
To thy fair competitor.

(*Exeunt; Bucholz, bowing. through one of the
vistas; and Frederic at one side.*)

(*The Scene changes.*)

ACT I.   Scene III.

An apartment in a Polish cottage, having a door in its centre.

———

Enter (by central door) Dzialinski, *who calls* Kollontay *in rather a loud whispering voice.*

Dzial.   Kollontay! Kollontay!—I say, come forth!
Disturb not Radziwilla; let her sleep.

Enter Kollontay.

Kol.   What now, my friend? tho' morn hath yet scarce
You find me ready to attend your call.   [ris'n,
Dzial.   O Kollontay, the enemy surround
Us on all sides.
Kol.   Heav'ns!—is it possible?
Dzial.   Hush! you'll disturb our consorts;—ere they rise,
I wish to have this conference with thee.
Kol.   Say on.
Dzial.   To crown our troubles, ev'ry hope hath fled
Of finding the Depôts where for five months
Our brother patriots conceal'd the arms.
Kol.   From what untoward cause can this proceed?
Dzial.   Those, who know where they are, while coming
Were intercepted by a Prussian force.   [hither
Kol.   And taken pris'ners?
Dzial.   Ev'n so; at Wloclawek, it was, this fell
Catastrophe occurr'd.

Kol. This is a *clincher*; it completely mars
  Our ev'ry prospect, and forebodes the worst.
  How long can we hold out?
Dzial. Perhaps not half a day.
Kol. How unpropitious!
Dzial. Tho', strongly barricaded as we are,
  We might repulse th' enemy till midnight.
Kol. If that be practicable, hear me *then* :—
  Let's give those Russian monsters no repose
  Throughout the live-long day. Hence, overcome
  By long fatigue, they'll early go to rest,
  Hoping to find us *here* by peep of day.
Dzial. Well?
Kol. We'll keep *unoccupied* a chosen few
  To pounce upon their sentinels at night,
  And cut them off; thus leaving us the pow'r
  To fly *securely*, when no hostile tongue
  Of all their guards shall live t' announce our exit.
Dzial. Ably suggested : if the onset fail,
  This glen shall be our refuge to the last;
  But, if the plan succeed, ere morning's dawn
  We'll leave those Muscovites free space to roam.

   (*A Russian trumpet is now heard from with-*
    out, sounding in the direction of one side,
    and immediately after another trumpet sounds
    in the direction of the other side. They an-
    swer each other with alternate blasts for some
    time, as from a considerable distance off.)

  Enter Radziwilla *and* Chrysillida, *in their morning*
      wrappers.

Chry. Dzialinski, what sounds are those we hear?
Dzial. (*feigning unconcern.*)
  Th' Muscovites, it seems, have got up early ;
     c 2

Or they've been up since late last night; they're fond
Of matin music, and withal invite
Their Polish neighbours to the warlike concert.

RADZ. (*to Chrysillida.*)
 Let us away, then, and equip ourselves
 To join this pastime by our husband's side.

CHRY. (*rubbing her eyes.*)
 We've slept *too* long, dear sister,—else the foe
 Had been *too* civil to disturb our rest.

RADZ. Come, therefore, without any more delay,
 And wipe thy slumb'ring eyelids in the field.

DZIAL. Tho' painful to announce, till midnight come,
 We feel oblig'd to leave you this retreat.

RADZ. Till midnight!

CHRY. Midnight! what has led to this?

DZIAL. 'Tis needless to conceal our present cares,
 So hear at once our motive, and be calm.
 Both the strong passes which command this glen
 Are in the foe's possession.

CHRY. Well! what of that?

DZIAL. This is to be by far the hottest day
 Of all the battles we have yet sustain'd.

CHRY. (*somewhat contemptuously.*)
 Go on!

DZIAL. We mean to give the enemy no rest
 For twenty hours.

CHRY. Proceed.

DZIAL. Exhausted and worn out, they'll gladly hail
 The period of repose.

CHRY. What more?

DZIAL. We'll keep a chosen band, till night reserv'd,
 To cut off all their sentinels, and fly
 From this ill-omen'd valley unperceiv'd.

CHRY. 'Tis well devis'd; and yet I cannot see

Why we should be your pris'ners all this day.

RADZ. Nor I, upon my honour! 'tis absurd
To keep us twenty hours in durance vile.

CHRY. Have we not shar'd your dangers from the first,
Happy to be where'er our consorts prov'd,
Tho' in the hottest of the battle's rage?
Is this, then, a fit period t' consign us
To nothing less than a dire pris'n! O shame!

DZIAL. We wish you to prepare for a long march
By due cessation from incessant toil

CHRY. Name it no more; our aggravated minds
Would kill us with suspense in half the time.

DZIAL. Take your own way, then, and acquit us freely
Of any wish to fetter those we love.

RADZ. Delightful fellows! Sister, come, retire,
And leave these morning wrappers far behind.

KOL. Well said, my gallant partner! shall I go
To help thy military habit on?

DZIAL. And I, Chrysillida, to aid thee, too?

CHRY. No, Polish chieftains, to your post repair;
Expect us in quick time, and keep the foe,
As you have ever kept him, *full in view!*

DZIAL. Heav'n guard you, best of women!

    (*Exeunt ; the two husbands by the central
door, the ladies at one side.*)

(*The Scene changes*)

ACT I.   Scene IV.

*Part of the City of Cracow, with the River Vistula running
through it.* [Note.—*The River Vistula flows from
Cracow (S.S.W.) down to Warsaw; these cities being
130 miles distant from each other.*] *Reiterated murmurs
of applause are first faintly heard; soon they grow louder
and louder, till at length they become general.*

———

Enter MADALINSKI *with a large body of troops; these duly
range themselves along the river.* KOSCIUSKO *sails up
it in a boat, and enters in the centre by landing; immediately after,*

MADAL.   Hail Kosciusko, hail!   Hail, Dictator
And Generalissimo of Poland!
            (*These words are echoed from a multitude of
            voices along the river, and in various direc-
            tions.   Kosciusko, on landing, shakes Mada-
            linski most cordially by the hand, and comes
            forward.*)
KOS.   Soldiers and Fellow Countrymen, I come,
Prepar'd to live or die with you; resolv'd
To join your Patriotic armaments
In raising Poland to her proper sphere,
Or else to forfeit life itself, and shed
Its *last, last* drop upon my country's hearse.
Yes, here I vow in presence of my God,—
In presence of both heav'n and earth,—where'er

A solemn or a sacred influence
Can actuate an honest, human heart,—
Never to sheathe my sword, till Freedom first
Regain her empire in my native land.
No other choice I make,—no other hope,—
No other thought endure. Receive me, then,
Not as your Tyrant to afflict you worse
Than openly avow'd hostility,
Nor as a Revolutionary Chief;
But as the *Guardian* of my country's rights,
To rescue Sov'reignty from foreign chains,—
To drive *invasion* to its northern *Den*,—
To knock off all your fetters,—set you free !
These once accomplish'd, your Dictator hence
His office shall resign, supremely bless'd
To see his Majesty again replac'd
On the proud eminence where free-born sway
Invests the Monarch with his people's love.
This be my purpose, motto, end, and aim ;
Be this my *longest* and my *last* intent !

> (*Here the loud bursts of applause are every-*
> *where renewed, and repeated huzzas rend the*
> *air. After they have subsided, he more*
> *particularly recognises Madalinski.*)

Brave Madalinski, I'm rejoic'd to see you !

MADAL. Honour'd Dictator, hail ! you see, my friend,
This trav'lling dust ; behold, I come from far !
We made our enemies support us well,—
Have rambl'd many a mile on Prussian cheer,
Nor stopp'd our journey since we left Pultusk.

KOS. 'Twas a bold measure, *somewhat premature*,
Save that the crisis left no room to pause.
The die is cast ; and nothing now remains
But to pursue the current where it glides.

MADAL. I lately had a mission to th' Empress.

KOS. Indeed!

MADAL. She took me for Oginski, and I bore
My novel title well; it serv'd to mask
My purpose with peculiar tact.

KOS. In a few days th' Imperial Dame returns
To Petersburg, where may she long remain!
But what impell'd you to her *Polish* Court?

MADAL. The King so importun'd me, I felt bound
To carry his petition to her feet.

KOS. Petition!—Poor fallen Stanislas!

MADAL. His suit is granted, and a regal storm
Is ready to assail him, right and left.

KOS. Just as conjectur'd; *crouching* only tempts
A persecuting Tyrant to grow worse.
How better would it be for Poland's King
To sit erect upon a hero's throne,
And bid defiance to a world in arms!

MADAL. That would indeed be better!

KOS. Tell me, have you any news from Warsaw?

MADAL. Its garrison, O chief, ere one short week
Are doom'd to be disbanded and disarm'd.

KOS. Disarm'd!

MADAL. On Easter Eve the Cossacks are to hold
All the chief stations, and in *Polish* cloaks,
To play us off with endless stratagems.

KOS. Is this a well authenticated fact?

MADAL. Kalinski is my author, who, it seems,
Has just deriv'd this sad intelligence
From one who's now at work on th' disguises.
Thus Russians, dress'd in Polish costume, are
To lay th' basis of our country's ruin.

KOS. Enough, enough; I need not wish to hear
Another word; the case is manifest;—

As long as Poland can the strength withhold
Of Cath'rine's ire, so long the Tyrant's brain
Will burn with inextinguishable malice.

MADAL. Nay, more; the fiendish Igolstrum himself
Hath ev'n presum'd to order the arrest
Of twenty most distinguish'd Senators.
Nor has he thought that outrage will suffice,
But hath commanded the grand General
To clear the citadels of all our troops.

KOS. Nay, hath the Muscovite presum'd so far?

MADAL. (*taking a letter out of his pocket, and presenting it to Kosciusko.*)
Here is a letter of that Minister,
Which, *intercepted,* I present to thee.
It shows the discomposure of his mind,
And indicates unmeasur'd violence
As likely to surround us on all sides.

KOS. (*taking the letter, and reading the superscription; now opening the letter, he reads the interior.*)

" To the Secretary at War
" at Petersburg.

" The whole Polish army, which musters
about 18,000 strong, is in complete rebellion,
excepting 4000, who compose the garrison of
Warsaw. Nor will it be either safe or expedient *to leave even these on their present footing.
Something most decisive must be done without
delay.* The insurrection strengthens every
moment, its progress is very rapid, and its
success terrifying. I am myself in expectation
of seeing the Confederation of Lublin advance;
and I have no hope but in God and the good
cause of my sovereign."

(*Ceasing to read.*)
How strange this language seems from such a source!
Here is a monster of iniquity,
Trampling all Laws both human and divine;
And yet this very fiend, this minister
Of ev'ry evil work, can dare to hope
That God will fight his battles and uphold
The cause of an imperial murderer.
But to proceed—
(*Here he resumes reading the letter.*)

    " Lithuania will not fail, certainly, to follow
the example."

(*Ceasing to read again.*)
     That surely need not be
A matter of surmise; the glorious flame
Of Patriotic ardour so pervades
That whole Palatinate from North to South.
 But come, my friends; no time is to be lost;
While gliding swiftly in our well-mann'd boats,
Our counsels we may hold with best effect.
   (*While they are retiring to the river, and pre-
paring to embark, the Curtain drops.*)

END OF THE FIRST ACT.

ACT II. SCENE I.

A wood with rocky defiles.

———

When the Curtain rises, the young PRINCE CHARLES *is seen
as if in earnest conversation with some Polish Soldiers
in the rear ground ; while, in front, the* PRINCESS
LUBOMIRSKI (*closely veiled*), *and* KOSCIUSKO *appear in
converse with each other.*

PRINCESS. Bear me, I pray you, till you hear me out !
Kos. (*aside.*)
        Her accents grow familiar to my ear ;
        I think I heard them many years ago ; [Madam,
        'Tis time t' unmask the lady. (*To her.*) Truly,
        This embassy will doubtless be a blind one,
        Except I see an end to this eclipse ;
        Leave, then, that lunar shadow,—and appear !
PRINCESS. (*aside.*)
        I greatly fear he recollects my voice.
(*To him.*) Permit me to proceed awhile unknown !
Kos.   No, madam, *that* I'll ne'er concede.
PRINCESS. Strong motives urge me to my present course.
Kos.   And strong incentives urge me, too.
PRINCESS. First *let* me speak !
Kos.   Not a word more, by Lucifer ! first show me
        Who thou art.
PRINCESS. Is this thy firm resolve ?

D

Kos.   Inflexible!

Princess. Then keep thy resolution, and behold!
            (*She now casts back her veil, and looks at him
                with much expression.*)

Kos. (*starting.*)
            What do I see? the Princess Lubomirski!
            Oh! let me shun her desolating presence!
                            (*Exit Kosciusko hastily.*)

Princess. (*sola.*)
            He's gone. And how could it be otherwise?
            The long-clos'd wound is open'd now afresh,
            And bleeds in all the ecstasy of grief.
            What shall I do? I've underta'en *too much.*
            Grant me, ye Guardian Pow'rs, sufficient nerve
            To hold the awful current of my course.

        Re-enter Kosciusko, *in front, in a state of reflection.*

Kos. (*aside.*)
            Yet why so senselessly precipitate?
            Shall Kosciusko from a woman fly,
            Altho' that woman be the very spouse
            Of his successful rival? No, no, no;—
            If she be a female luminary,—
            Her beams, with her virginity, have fled,
            Leaving behind them to transfix my breast
            Not ev'n the *twilight* of her *former pow'r*
                            (*Turning round and addressing her.*)
            Madam, behold how soon the bird returns
            To the skill'd Archer's snare.   Be not surpris'd
            If this our meeting under such extremes
            Of *unexpected* pleasure, may perplex.
            Excuse me, Madam,—but I thought I knew

Myself far better. Yet with all our pride
Thy sex can awe us with superior grace.

PRINCESS. Hold, Sir;—I hope in these few hasty words
There's nothing like returning to the chase.
Remember, I am *not* my own ;—*another*
Calls me his; and his I'll be for ever!

KOS. I understand you, Madam ; and, to prove
My insight to your thoughts, you mean to say
'Twould be a miserable enterprise
To beat about another's lair for prey ;
To feed, in fact, on what is long enjoy'd
E'en by a rival;—that were *poor* indeed!
Too poor, I also ween, for him who now
Addresses thee; not that he boasts of aught
To please a *Princess*, but that he disdains
The smiles of fell dishonour ev'n from *thee.*

PRINCESS. This is sufficient to confirm my mind
In ev'ry sentiment so long indulg'd :
If genuine honour gilds a human heart,
That *heart* in Kosciusko ever beats.

KOS. Did he not love thee? think thee ray'd in light?
And challenge all Creation to surpass thee?
Where'er he wander'd, did he hope t' explore
So pure an image, or with truth more grac'd?
With loveliness, with dignity, with worth,
With ev'ry blandishment that really lives
Or fancy could create? Nay, here not pleas'd
To ruminate o'er earthly excellence,
Thought he this globe not half refin'd for thee?
Look'd he still higher? to a higher Zone
Still wing'd his flight, to see if aught, so fair
As thou, were giv'n to other Spheres? But ah!
'Twas all a dream,—an idle, transient dream ;
So he awoke, Madam, and found thee fled.

A monument of female fickleness,—
Unamiable, undignified, untrue,
Well form'd to play on man's credulity,
And with a versatility unmatch'd
Develope how the wind can change its course.
With such strong facts remember'd to this hour,
By what infatuation hast thou sought
This poignant interview? what led thee on?
Was there no other female on the earth
To undertake this mission save thyself?

PRINCESS. O Kosciusko, is it thus you treat
A visitor like me? is it for this
I left my Lithuanian Domicile?
For thee and for my Country to assuage,
If possible, the proud Tzarina's ire?
Into some milder current to direct
The petulance of conquest? or to plead
At least sincerely for my native land?
Just as the new-rear'd constitution smil'd
And threw her hallow'd mantle o'er the realm,
Who could behold the fairy vision pass
Evaporating at the era of its birth?
Was it for me, or aught with conscious soul,
To witness such calamity *unmov'd*,
Shunning the cares of Patriotic toil,
In the vile sloth of Slavery unnerv'd?
No, Kosciusko, I would erst invite
Dangers in ev'ry quarter of the Globe,—
Whether o'er ocean, or the desert's track,—
O'er the parched horrors of a torrid Zone,—
Or where the chilling frost's incessant empire
Mid bars of ice confines the frozen earth.
No terror should impede me,—floods nor storms,
Nor all the restless Elements of ire

That ever thunder'd o'er the race of man.
One vast impediment alone appears
That could divert me from my firm resolve ;—
And need I tell thee what that barrier is,
So long as Death his mortal Sceptre holds ?

Kos.   If Patriotic ardour in my breast
Were like a lamp going out, then wouldst thou serve
To blow it in again :—one vital gale
From such a charmer, would rekindle all ;—
All, (do you mind me ?) but the latent spark
Of former *love* and *evanescent dreams*.
These, nor the rudest blast that ever howl'd,
Nor hurricanes, nor tempests, nor the trump
Of universal chaos come again,
Could wake to aught but ghastly influence,
Or pale Existence ready to expire.
Like a damp vapour, it would serve to chill
The very ray that brought it into being.

PRINCESS. Mistake not, Kosciusko, (tho' there still
Is music in that War-fam'd honour'd name!)
Mistake me not, proud warrior, I nor come
To kindle what would now be criminal,
Nor under any circumstances, fan
A flame, as you admit, almost extinct.
No ; for far other purposes I come,—
To serve my Country, and her name restore
Amid the *free-born* Kingdoms of the World !

Kos. (*aside.*)
Hah ! I am hit again ;—her Patriot fire
Is e'en more irresistible than love ;—
I must forgive her, tho' my breast still bleeds
With the sad wounds inflicted by her hand.

(*To her.*) Most gen'rous heroine ! mine were hasty words ;
You've nearly vanquish'd me a second time :

You teach me to obliterate all sense
Of former injuries,—and only think
Of that ennobled passion which sustains
The love of Country burning in our breasts
Like a pure Vestal flame that shuns all gross
Corporeal aliment ;—that lives, aye *lives*
On mind, on thought, on essence, and on soul,—
Congenial Spirit of *undying* fame
That seeks to flourish in *immortal* bloom!

PRINCESS. Oh! 'tis a theme whereon, I knew full well,
We always fed congenial sentiments :
And, trusting to that nobleness innate
That ever actuates the truly brave,
I thought *you could forgive*, and e'en unite
The humble Counsels of a penitent
With thy superior knowledge of mankind.
Thus, led to throw myself on your chaste ire,
That mingles with compassion ev'ry frown,
I come, on perilous adventure bent,
Resolv'd t' endure defeat in ev'ry form,
If not to triumph in the cause of Freedom!

KOS.   Go, then, dear Princess,—while there yet is hope,
Strain ev'ry nerve in the great cause. Who knows
What female Eloquence may yet effect ?
If thou deliv'rest from an early tomb
The new-fram'd Constitution of this realm,—
The work of three bright legislative years
That would have *rescued* Poland from the Gulf
Of fell oppression, anarchy, and ruin,—
That would have plac'd her where she ought to be,
On the bright pinnacle of liberty,—
An ornament to nations, bless'd on earth,
While water'd with the dews from heav'n above :
If thou canst put a key-stone to this arch

Of national resuscitation, or,
(O glorious undertaking!) nobly rear
The prostrate column of our Country's hopes :—
Then wilt thou live in joy's supreme career
The proud preserver of thy native land.
Go, Princess, go ;—do this,—and live for ever!

> *(Exeunt; Kosciusko at one side, in front;
> while the Princess Lubomirski, retiring and
> taking the young Prince Charles by the hand,
> makes her exit (with him) far back in the
> rear ground.)*

(The Scene changes.)

ACT II. Scene II.

A wood, with King Frederic's Prussian Tent at one side.

———

Enter (in front) Igolstrum, *disguised in a Polish cloak.*

Igols. (*solus.*)
 What! Madalinski so receiv'd by Fred'ric!
 He who first rais'd the standard of revolt,—
 To be so honour'd by the Prussian King!—
 How truly unaccountable!—'Tis well
 T'arrive thus unobserv'd,—the better far
 To probe, unseen, in this disguis'd attire,
 What otherwise I could not hope to learn.
 Thither they come. Near yonder tent, it seems,
 Some useful information might be gain'd;
 Let me retire, then, and with caution mark
 The real character of friend and foe.
   · (*Igolstrum, in the rear, goes near the Tent
   to listen.*)

Enter (in front) Frederic *and* Madalinski.

Madal. What has your Majesty t' fear from Russia?
Fred. Oh! nothing, positively nothing!—
Madal. And with auxiliaries so far renown'd
   As Prussia might confer, if thus allied,—

What hath our Stanislas to apprehend,
Back'd by his own brave People! they who never
Quitted his royal standard ;—and who still
But follow the Dictator, to secure
His Sceptre and the *Dominion* of the laws?

FRED. I must admit,—in such a strange position
As between opposite extremes he held,—
No nation could have prov'd more truly loyal,
Or more devoted to an injur'd King.

MADAL. Is it not strange, then, he could ever crouch
To Cath'rine's unrelenting violence?
Casting the new and admirable code
Of Polish legislation to the winds?
What! are the laws of *Ninety-one* to be
For ever trampl'd underneath *her* foot,—
The *very foot* that trampled on *his* Crown,
And spurn'd the obligation of an Oath
With sacrilegious transport, rage, and war?—
Is the Tzarina thus to rule us all,
And *banish liberty* from *ev'ry* clime?

FRED. Come, Madalinski, Patriotic Zeal
May carry thee *too* far ;—let us reserve
This subject for a more convenient time.
Poor Stanislas! his feelings are acute ;—
He's a most kind and well-intention'd Sov'reign,
And hospitality from me demands
A studious delicacy at this crisis.
E'en on my own dull sensibility
Thou hast not fail'd to operate ; nor till
The present could I think myself so soft.
Nevertheless, my tears are soon exhal'd
Like dews before the sun of reason's pow'r.

MADAL. 'Twere well, indeed, if her effulgence shone
More than it does upon the race of man ;—

'Twould banish *half* th' injustice of the world,
And soften the remainder into mercy.

FRED.   Pond'ring so many most important points,
No trifling difficulty reigns around.
On one hand Polish Freedom claims her share ;
On th' other the *security* of States.
Here the new Polish Constitution pleads ;—
There the due Poise of Kingdoms cries—beware !
Here the increase of Revolutions frown ;—
There the stability of Governments,
And all their firmly constituted forms.

My feelings, I admit, are in *your* favour,
So beauteous is the garb of liberty !—
Yet, for that *great* concession, you will find
My better reason on the other side.
How sorrowful it *is*,—in this review
My head and heart can never go together !
I'm like a lover warring night and day
Against the moral empire of his mind.
Yet, as th' attachment cannot be dissolv'd,
I must contemplate future offices
Of kindness to the object of my love.
Tell Kosciusko, therefore, how I'm held,
As if in social, matrimonial bonds,
To his dear Country ;—while all other ties
Are seeking a Divorce against my will.

      (*Exeunt Frederic and Madalinski in opposite
         directions.   Igolstrum comes forward un-
         perceived by them.*)

IGOLS. (*solus.*)

I know not what to think of these events ;—
King Fred'ric, certainly, seems insincere.
Let pregnant time, however, solve the rest.
Now to remove this Vesture of disguise,

And seek an audience of th' Prussian Monarch.
As for this Madalinski, he shall soon
Become my Pris'ner, as of late devis'd.
The Empress is resolv'd to recognise
No embassy that comes from such a source.
Hence, at his exit from this Royal Camp,
A troop of Cossacks, station'd near at hand,
Shall give him salutation *well impress'd*, —
Tho' diff'ring far from his reception *here*.

                    (*Exit Igolstrum.*)

           (*The Scene changes.*)

ACT II.   Scene III.

*A wood in a glen, having the River Vistula running through
it. Considerably elevated is a rocky passage winding
out of sight, and having a very rude parapet about three
feet in height. So much of this parapet is visible as
would occupy the circumference of a large tower's base;
and the parapet itself rests on a lofty ledge of rocks which
hang over the river. For brevity, this entire projecting
ledge is called the* Promontory.

*This Scene commences with a vast noise proceeding from a
Cavern behind the promontory, where at length a huge
rock is driven forward by Russian miners who are working
within the Cave. Thus a fissure is made therein,
through which some of the miners become visible.*

Enter Suwarrow, *with some difficulty, through the fissure
thus made, followed by two or three Russian miners.
Standing foremost on the promontory, he takes a very
exploring view in every direction.*

Suwar. Bravely done, my fine fellows!—this secures
  Our wary prey. Go to the new-found Cave,
  And thence despatch a trusty messenger
  To both the Passes,—to renew the siege
  In both positions with united force.
  Away!———
    (*Exeunt miners (above) into the cavern.*)

Thus to withdraw the foe's attention,
Will leave us here an unmolested course
Till we invade them where they least suspect.
                              (*Looking to one side.*)
But who are these that hither bend their way?—
There's something most peculiar in their dress;
What, if they prove th' heroines of this vale?—
Let me be seated on this lofty rock
To hear them eulogize me, as they 're wont.
        (*He sits down, having his head merely visible,*
        to the audience, over the parapet.)

Enter (*below*), *in converse,* RADZIWILLA *and* CHRYSILLIDA.

RADZI. The happy period of deliverance
        Is not so readily foreseen in war.
CHRY.   I'm growing weary of this painful pris'n.
        Merciful heav'ns!—how long are we to be
        The sport of that Suwarrow's fell desires?
RADZI. I wonder if a woman gave him birth?
CHRY.   Judging from his malign propensities
        And blood-stain'd track,—we never should suppose
        That human nature led him into life.
        From Tartarus alone the canine fiend
        Could date his origin,—whelp'd in the midst
        Of Furies, and sent up to mortal light
        To darken all our prospects, and diffuse
        A gloomy pestilence where'er he moves.
SUWAR. (*unheard by them.*)
        Thank you, kind ladies!—You have doubtless gain'd
        My gratitude.   Be well assur'd I only
        Wait the earliest opportunity
        To give you salutation in due form.

                        E

RADZI. Come, dearest sister, let us now ascend
The rocky way that overhangs th' river,
Thence to behold this valley's eastern pass,
And learn what ever-restless time presents
While starry Hesperus prepares to smile.

CHRY. O may he smile from his celestial sphere
With happy omens!—and ere morn unfold
The path to liberation from this glen!
Come, Radziwilla.

(*Exeunt Chrysillida and Radziwilla.*)

SUWAR. (*standing up on the Promontory.*)
Now, by th' Gemini!—the doves are coming
Into my very lap. What shall I do?—
I think myself an overmatch for both.
'Twould be unmanly, therefore, to require
In this position an auxiliar force.
The fame, besides, of taking such a pair
With my own proud and unaided prowess,
Will make my tow'ring plume as much admir'd
By Venus and Lucina, as by Mars.

(*Looking towards one side.*)

Egad, I see a most convenient nook
Whence, couching like a lion, I might spring
Upon my long-lov'd prey with best effect.

(*Exit above. Trumpets now sound first at
one side and afterwards at the other side,
as if from a considerable distance off. A
tremendous cannonade soon follows, which is
similarly heard, as from a scene of action
somewhat remote, in each of opposite directions. After some time elapses, the distant
cannonade dies away. Several loud shrieks
are now heard; and a clashing of swords
ensues.*)

Re-enter RADZIWILLA *and* CHRYSILLIDA, *on the Promontory, sword in hand.*

CHRY.   What a tremendous onset!

RADZ.   Had he not fallen down that steep, I fear
No earthly arm could save us from his ire.

CHRY.   He is not vanquish'd *yet;*—hence let us hurl
Our cloaks away,—they so encumber us.
 Watch, Sister, dear, while I throw mine over.
       (*Chrysillida takes off her cloak, and throws it
        over the Promontory.*)
Now, Radziwilla, I shall watch for *thee.*
       (*Radziwilla does the same with her cloak.
        Both their cloaks fall below on the land by
        the river's side.*)

RADZ.   If he rally, and we become disarm'd,
What shall we do?

CHRY.   Do?

RADZ.   Yes.

CHRY.   Why,—let me think. I have it.

RADZ.   Reveal it quick as thought itself.

CHRY.   Let us retreat along this winding way.

RADZ.   It is so narrow and terrific.

CHRY.   So much the better;—that's our only chance;—.
If he attempt it,—the huge Buffalo
Will fall into the water and be drown'd.

RADZ.   He comes again;—lo, there he is!

CHRY.   How much he limps! his tumble was severe.

RADZ.   I think we'll both be able for him *now.*

Re-enter, on the Promontory, SUWARROW, *sword in hand.*

SUWAR.   Ladies, 'tis best to yield at once.

CHRY.   Never!

RADZ. No, never!

SUWAR. Then with reluctance to renew my suit
In this persuasive manner,—mark how soon
I'll shiver both your swords to atoms.

> (*He engages them both, and first succeeds in
> hurling Radziwilla's sword out of her hand
> over the Promontory: it falls below on the
> land at the river's side. Suwarrow desists,
> and again tries to parley.*)

SUWAR. 'Tis madness to persist;—so now confess
Yourselves my pris'ners, or beware.

CHRY. Go, Radziwilla, round, as we resolv'd.

RADZ. I'll never quit thee, Sister, till I die.

CHRY. Then stand behind me. (*to Suwarrow*) Monster,
why delay?

SUWAR. Poh!—'tis a vain attempt;—put up thy blade.

> (*Chrysillida makes a sudden dash at him, and
> an obstinate encounter takes place. At
> length he proves equally successful, whirling
> the sword out of her hand, also, which
> follows that of Radziwilla. She now (as it
> were) fixes her eyes on some object behind
> Suwarrow.*)

CHRY. 'Tis gone;—Ha! but who are these a-coming?

> (*Suwarrow turns round, and looks earnestly
> for some seconds in the same direction.
> Meanwhile, both the sisters seize this oppor-
> tunity, and rush round the Promontory,
> and so* Exeunt, above.)

SUWAR. I can see nothing.

> (*At length turning about and perceiving them
> gone.*)

'Tis a stratagem.
By gingo, that is clever;—ready wit

Hath giv'n these Amazonians time to fly.
I'll try to follow them.
  (*He goes partly round the Promontory, yet*
   still in view.)
      Heav'ns! what a depth!
Like flags of truce, they wave their handkerchiefs.
O horrible! they're going;—down they fall
Into the angry flood. Now borne along
Its rapid waters,—strange to tell, they float;—
They're still upon the surface of th' current.
Ah! there they go; its rapid windings whirl
Those victims out of sight. I fear they're lost.
Poor creatures, fare ye well! I'm greatly griev'd;
My conscience almost smites me for this dire
And madly unforeseen calamity.
  (*He returns before the fissure, while speaking*
   the last three lines. Exit Suwarrow, above,
   into the Cave behind the Promontory.)

Enter DZIALINSKI, below. *During the former part of the*
following Soliloquy, he moves across the Stage.

DZIAL. (*solus*).
  The dreadful cannonade, which this day roar'd,
Hath terribly disjointed all our planks.
I greatly fear the siege is near an end,
And a dire massacre to end us all.
  (*Looking downward, he perceives the cloaks and*
   swords of Radziwilla and Chrysillida.)
But what are these?
  (*He takes up the cloaks, one in each hand.*)
      I'm lost in dire conjectures.
Their swords, too, lie before me! let me see.
  (*The cloaks fall from his hands, and he takes*
   up the swords, closely examining them.)
     E 2

Oh! it is *too, too* true! mysterious fact!
What! are they murder'd?—drown'd or, O far
Have they been led into captivity?—   [worse!—
Great God! where can I find a key t' open
The dark and dismal portals of their fate?—
But lo! here comes,—O lacerating thought!
Perhaps—my *follow widower*—in woe.

Enter KOLLONTAY, *followed by a company of Polish Soldiers,
who range themselves along the side whereat they enter.*

O Kollontay, behold this well-known falchion!
    (*He shows him Chrysillida's sword.*)

KOL.   Good Heav'ns!—Dzialinski, what is it?—
DZIAL.   Look at it.
KOL.   As I do live,—it is Chrysillida's!—   .
DZIAL.   Aye,—there it is,—but where—O where is she?—
KOL.   My boding soul's already on the rack!
DZIAL.   Look, also, at this scimitar.
    (*He now shows him the other sword.*)

KOL.   Hah! 'tis Radziwilla's! *Now, now,* my friend,
The blackest sable seems our doom.
DZIAL.   (*dropping both the swords*).
O ye pow'rs! why have we liv'd so long?
To reach this awful chasm of dark despair!
KOL.   Yet, let me think:—perchance they still survive.
DZIAL.   O happy thought!—*too happy*—to be true!
KOL.   I am so vastly stunn'd,—I'm quite unnerv'd,—
Completely paralys'd from head to foot.
DZIAL.   I wish I could believe them *still alive!*
KOL.   Come, let us seek them wheth'r in life or death.
DZIAL.   Where, Kollontay?   [wood;
KOL.   Take half these men, and with them search yon

Let th' rest follow me in this direction.
Go, Dzialinski,—rouse thyself,—be firm.

(*Exit Kollontay, followed by several file of
Polish Soldiers.*)

DZIAL. Come, valiant countrymen,—I'll try to lead you,
Altho' despondency hath quite unmann'd me.
Yes, yes;—where *are* they,—noblest of their sex?
Is there no friendly spirit near at hand
To whisper it upon the rueful breeze?
O my Chrysillida!—where shall I find thee?
My heart!—my mind!—my very brain's on fire!!

(*Exit Dzialinski, similarly accompanied with
Soldiers as Kollontay, but in opposite directions.*)

(*Enter a boat rowed by six men, conveying two
ladies in a reclining posture. It is rowed
slowly and completely across, and Exits.*)

(*Trumpets sound again, as if remote; followed
by a somewhat distant cannonade, which
after the lapse of some time dies away.*)

Re-enter SUWARROW, *above, through the fissure from the
cavern. He stands on the Promontory, as before.*

SUWAR. (*solus.*)

All now seems ripe for harvest; we'll begin
To mow th' fields of battle in right earnest.
I wonder what reception these mad Poles
Will give the Prussians that, in thirteen barks,
Have actually sail'd into this glen.
I hope they rescued the *fair divers*, who
So resolutely fought me hand in hand.
"Tho' *in the midst of Furies* I was *whelp'd*,"
I feel an int'rest in their preservation.

(*Speaking to the miners within the fissure.*) .
    Widen this breach, ye miners ;—else in vain
    Will all your labours be :—'twill scarce admit
    A single man to pass,—much less an army.
    Tug, tug away, then, as if all your lives
    Depended on the issue ; haste, be brisk ;—
    It must be finish'd ere the midnight hour.
            (*Here the Curtain immediately drops.*)

          END OF THE SECOND ACT.

ACT III.   Scene I.

*A wood not far from Warsaw, with the River Vistula running
through it, and having a Bridge over it.*

———

Kosciusko *is discovered at the head of his Army accompanied
by Artillery.*

Kos.   Soldiers, it well becomes you thus to keep
  The enemy before you.   They prefer
  To be your pioneers, and clear your way.
  They're e'en more vigilant in that respect,
  Than our own people ;—with such active strides
  They strut before you on the wings of flight.
  But here comes Dzialinski ;—how well-timed !

Enter Dzialinski.

  Welcome, illustrious chieftain !—briefly tell me,
  Are the bands of Sieradz *yet* equipp'd ?
Dzial. They are, most honour'd and rever'd Dictator.
  Now fully arm'd with Prussian musketry
  And ammunition from the captur'd barks,—
  They're ready for the field, and nobly pant
  To dash like thunder at th' astonish'd foe.
Kos.   Noble fellows !—with such auxiliaries
  The very crest of war might well be proud.
Dzial. They 've gain'd some slight advantages already,
  And look with ardour to the coming storm.

Kos.   But tell me, Dzialinski, how thy spouse
        And Radziwilla bear their late afflictions ?—
        From all I've heard, they had not long to live,
        When brave Dombrouski to their rescue came.

Dzial. If his arrival met the least delay,
        They *both* had been irrevocably lost.

Kos.   The Russians' favourable error, too,
        Is still a subject of profound surprise,—
        Permitting all your armaments to fly
        Without the least obstruction on *their* part.

Dzial. Seeing the barges were of Prussian form,
        They unmolested suffer'd them to pass,
        Inconscious of their *capture*, or *how mann'd.*
        At Wlocklawek, it was, they had been seiz'd,
        By an heroic Lithuanian force;—
        This to Suwarrow haply was unknown,
        Who took them for the ships of his allies.

Kos.   You left him, therefore, a deserted glen.

Dzial. Whoever saw the monster enter it,
        And bellow thro' the void his loud disdain,
        With vast amusement must have heard the fiend
        Venting his anger on Vacuity.

Kos.   We cannot be too thankful for the past,
        Inspiring, as it does, such future hopes.

Dzial. My Lord Dictator, I regret to cast
        A single shade around our bright'ning prospects;—
        But there are worse, far worse than open foes.

Kos.   How ?

Dzial. Th' foes, of whom I speak, are odious brawlers.
        They 've so inflam'd the foolish populace,
        That all our prisons have been madly forc'd,
        And, horrid to relate, a multitude
        Of unoffending captives put to death.

Kos.   What ! butcher'd in cold blood ?——

DZIAL. A Massacre more barbarous or base
Ne'er curs'd the annals of the wildest climes.

Kos. O fell perdition! that, indeed, 's a source
Of foul hostility more truly dire,
Than all the enemies we ever met
In war's extreme tempestuous career!
What will our neighbour states declare? what will
Surrounding nations? what *all Europe* say?—

DZIAL. 'Twere better far to lose a hundred fights,—
Or twenty battles in a single day,
Than have so foul a stigma thus impress'd
On Freedom's Glorious Cause!

Kos. Oh! 'tis too much to think of! it will drive
Me mad. 'Twill be a wonder, if one friend
Be left e'en among ourselves. But tell me,
While this was doing, were ye all asleep?—

DZIAL. It came so like an unforewarn'd deluge,—
Dark desolation roll'd around us all,
Before we knew the evil of the times.

Kos. Have they been executed?

DZIAL. No.

Kos. No!——

DZIAL. Not *yet;*—the Council wait thy Signature
To put the Law in force.

Kos. Give me the warrant!—aye, and if they had
A myriad lives to lose,—inglorious death
Shall visit them before the setting sun.

DZIAL. Ere it be sign'd, I've promis'd to apply
E'en in behalf of one of thine own friends.

Kos. What! I a friend among that odious band!

DZIAL. With deep contrition he implores thy mercy.

Kos. I do not wish to know his very name,—
At least till I do *something* for my *friend!*
Yes; hear me,—he shall have the privilege

Of being th' first to die;—mark me, I say,
The *very first* to *expiate* his crimes
On the avenging scaffold of his country.
Give me the warrant.
                    (*He takes the Warrant from Dzialinski.*)
(*aloud.*)   Send a Drummer here
With pen and ink.   I'll sign it like a Soldier
On the drum head itself;—and then, my friend,
My *real friend*, let not the very winds
Be swifter than thy course, to give despatch
To this same act of justice to mankind.

> (*Enter two drummers, one carrying a drum
> in his hand, and the other a pen and ink.
> Kosciusko begins to read the death-warrant
> with great rapidity, starts at one part of it
> in particular, and after reading, signs it on
> the drum-head.   Meanwhile, in front, in
> reflection with himself,*)

DZIAL.   Tho' to fulfil my promise I resolv'd,—
I knew the just Dictator would not spare
The nearest relative he had on earth.
The crime, too, is so villainous, I felt
The shame of self-reproach to advocate,
E'en in th' slightest and most feeble manner,
The liberation of a fiend so base.

> (*Here Kosciusko comes forward, and in very
> expressive silence returns the death-warrant
> to Dzialinski, adding a signal with his hand
> for the instant departure of the latter.*)

> (*Exit Dzialinski, at the same side whereat
> he entered.   Here Kosciusko looks upward,
> clasps his hands with evident symptoms of
> internal affliction, and moves slowly to the*

*side opposite to that whereat Dzialinski just
made his exit.   In that point,)*

Enter KOLLONTAY, *accidentally meeting him there.*

Kos.   Hah! Kollontay,—hast thou heard th' horrid news?

KOL.   'Tis truly dire.

Kos.   'Tis infamous.

KOL.   It baffles all my calculations.

Kos.   'Tis damnable.

KOL.   Very unworthy conduct for an Empress.

Kos.   An Empress!

KOL.   Yes, she, it was, who order'd him in chains.

Kos.   Him!—in chains!—why, what is here?

KOL.   I thought you knew th' entire transaction;—hear.
    As Madalinski was returning home
    From Fred'ric's royal camp,—he was entrapp'd
    And made a pris'ner by a Russian band.

Kos.   Oh, then, 'tis manifest we *both* have news,
    Of very diff'rent import in the main.
    Thou speak'st of one catastrophe, and, lo,
    I of anoth'r.   What! my ambassador
    Imprison'd! cast in chains! This be my first,
    Immediate object.   Know'st thou where he is?

KOL.   Yes, in the castle where the Empress now
    Enjoys her pastime during her sojourn.

Kos.   'Tis a *fit prison* for my honour'd friend.
    But come, we'll visit this *imperial gaoler,*
    And countermand th' warrant of detention.

(aloud.) Let th' whole army *now* be put in motion;
    Nor leave one single cannon in reserve.
    Take all your batt'ring train; and follow me.

F

(*To Kollontay.*)

As we proceed, my friend, I've other ills
To tell thee of, will reach thine inmost pore.

> (*Exeunt* (*in a direction opposite to that which Dzialinski took*) *both Kosciusko and Kollontay, followed by the Polish army and artillery, &c.*)

(*The Scene changes, while they are filing off.*)

ACT III. Scene II.

An apartment, in a Polish Castle, having in its rear a central door.

———

Enter the Empress Catherine, *the* Princess Lubomirski, *and* Suwarrow.

Suwar.   Your Majesty already knows my thoughts.
Cath.   What! have my late commands produc'd no
   (*To him aside.*)   [change?
         In presence of the Princess, mark me well!—
         I wish thee to assume a milder tone.
Suwar. (*aside, to Catherine.*)
         And play the hypocrite?—that's not *my* way.
Cath. (*aside, to herself.*)
         The brute's inflexible.
Suwar.   Besides, I hate the Lubomirski race,
   (*Aside, to Catherine.*)
         And have good reason for my present humour.
   (*Aside, to himself.*)
         Nor do I yet forget that odious glen,
         Where I was so insulted and cajol'd;—
         An *empty* valley was a *fine reward*
         For such a tiresome and laborious siege.
Princess. Perhaps the Empress hath some private hints
         To give her Gen'ral,—which my presence mars.
                  (*The Princess is about to retire.*)
Cath.   Not in the least, dear Princess, do not go.

    Suwarrow lo ! the Princess Lubomirski,
    Deputed by her Consort, hath essay'd
    T' avert my anger from his erring race.
    What are thy counsels, then ?—the more desir'd,
    As thou hast led our battles to this hour,
    And know'st th' temper that prevails in Poland.

SUWAR. Experience teaches that the restless Poles
    Are never tractable,—except in war.

PRINCESS. Yes, I admit the fact;—nor ever will,
    While fell injustice goads them on t' battle.

CATH. Injustice, Princess ?—where would'st thou direct
    That solemn imputation ?

PRINCESS. On three confederated royal pow'rs
    Who erst in turn to victory aspir'd
    Partly by means of Polish valour won.
    And what was our reward ? by those we serv'd,
    And in the scale of nations higher rais'd,
    T' have been *neglected merely* had been light
    Compar'd with the result :—*our* recompense
    Was not *neglect*, but *anxious looking after*
    Till you *Dismember'd* our unhappy realm.

CATH. The cause of that Dismemberment, thou know'st,
    Embraced a train of most efficient reasons.
    Partly from ancient title,—and in part
    To put the cause of Revolution down,—
    Necessity, with ancient rights, combin'd
    To circumscribe thy nation in due bounds.

PRINCESS. Wisdom, no doubt, seeks to be justified
    By all her children ;—hence her name abus'd
    Is sometimes giv'n to rapine, robbery,
    Iniquity, oppression ;—all in turn
    Can claim *expediency* in their behalf.

CATH. I wish to treat thee as thy rank suggests,
    So measure thine expressions with reserve.

PRINCESS. Measure thy policy with justice first.

CATH. What is the object thou hast *now* in view ?—

PRINCESS. T' induce thee to relinquish that dire sway
Which only makes thee like a tyrant seem,
Doing *thee* little service, while o'er *us*
It shakes the iron sceptre of despair !

CATH. If time permitted, truth perhaps could say
Enough to justify the course I took.

PRINCESS. Excuse me, madam, but I blame thee much
For not doing justice to thy very self.

CATH. I do not understand you.

PRINCESS. Suppose you made us *love* thee, whereas now—

CATH. You *hate* me, *I* suppose.

PRINCESS. 'Tis well conjectur'd, whatsoever source
It springs from.

CATH. You compliment me, madam ;—rest assur'd
I'm not offended at the candid truth.
Besides, too, I'm no advocate for love,
Where my *admirers* would be *masters* also.

PRINCESS. Masters ! Of what ?—Of their *own* native land ?
Could this offend an honest neighb'ring state ?

CATH. Yes,—as a foolish neighbour's house on fire
Would threat'n destruction to my own repose.
My earliest care would be to quench the flame,
And save both mansions from untimely ruin.

PRINCESS. So far as simple preservation goes,
The truth 's admitted ; but, the flame extinct,
Could it be thought an ornament to close
Our windows up in future, and exclude
The blessings of that light to all vouchsaf'd ?

CATH. That is not your condition ; Poland breathes
As much the air of freedom as ourselves.

PRINCESS. But *all are slaves ;* Whereas by nature's laws
Fair liberty 's the birthright of mankind.

CATH. (*aside.*)

> I do not like this subject ; 'tis to *me*
> At all times most unwelcome, most unwise.
> Let me, then, change it by a happy ruse!
> (*To Suwarrow.*)
> Suwarrow, speak ; can we in future hope
> To be *less hated* by these *restless* Poles ?—

SUWAR. Never, O mighty Empress, till they die,—

> Or thou becom'st as *foolish* as themselves.

PRINCESS. (*to Suwarrow.*)

> Unlike a Statesman, thou can'st ne'er aspire
> To *free-born* empire ; warfare yields the food
> With which alone thine appetite seems pleas'd.

SUWAR. (*aside.*)

> Now for an ample field of just revenge!
> (*To the Princess.*)
> I thank thee, madam ;—nothing is more true ;
> I love luxuriant fields manur'd by death.
> Did not the race of Islam do their worst
> To give *my* carcase to their birds of prey ?—
> Why, then, should I be squeamish, over-nice
> To kill by measure, lenity, or rule ?—
> No ;—let me stride o'er ev'ry foolish thought,
> And hail th' scent of carnage like a nosegay !
> Doth golden Ceres cheer the neighing horse
> With vital corn ? so is a crop of blood
> A prospect worthy of a warrior bold.

PRINCESS. (*aside.*)

> The fell barbarian !—Nero seems to rise,
> Again to desolate the human race ;—
> Or if we see a diff'rence in them, lo !
> The present demon is a Russian fiend,
> Whereas the other was a Roman scourge.

CATH. (*aside.*)

> Much as I feel chagrin'd, I'll give him scope

To treat this Princess as she best deserves;—
She's certainly *appall'd*, and well hath *earn'd* it,
Her late assurance rose to such a height.

PRINCESS. (*aside.*)

Th' Empress shows some symptoms of displeasure,
I'll tempt him, therefore, to perplex her more.

(*To him.*) Is there no mercy in thy warlike code
For mourning brides,—or orphans bath'd in tears?

SUWAR. (*aside.*)

O that curs'd glen!—it still excites my rage.

CATH. (*aside.*)

That question seems to discompose him much;—
I wonder will he answer it?

SUWAR. (*aside.*)

Her hateful interrogatory brings
That empty valley into view again.
Yet, she'll never muzzle me; I'd die first.

(*To the Princess.*)

As to their orphans,—we might send them *home.*
Not so the bridal captives;—these might prove
Attractive, and far other thoughts inspire.
Nay,—if an en'my hath a blooming bride,—
Oh! how delicious 'tis to kill him soon,
And kiss his widow o'er his very bier!
Take me, then, Madam, as thy fancy wills:—

(*To Catherine.*)

And thou, great Empress! view me, at a call,
Ready to do thy bidding, and transfix
Man, woman, child,—and in one tomb immerse,
To give thine enemies a long repose.

CATH. (*aside.*)

Confusion seize the monster!—he'd undo [sels.
Th' best-plann'd, wisest, and most prudent coun-

(*To him.*) Suwarrow, thou hast shock'd me; ruthless man,

I know not what to think. If this be war,
I'm sure I've no desire to cultivate
So great a horror, so profound a scourge.

(*Exit Catherine.*)

SUWAR. (*aside.*)

So she's decamp'd; I'll follow her this instant,
And try to soften her imperial ire.

PRINCESS. (*as he is going off, interrupting his retreat.*)

Stop, Sir, awhile, and hear what *I've* to say.
Thou that delight'st so much in shedding blood,—
Dost thou imagine that thyself wast made
Invulnerable or invincible ?
Know'st thou not Polish valour ? and that thou,
Much as renown'd for conquest, yet may'st die ?

SUWAR. Pshaw, madam, I'm so busy in the field,
I have not time to think of life or death,
At least in *your way ; mine* is to revolve
Thro' scenes of devastation,—with no care
Save that of killing ev'ry foe I meet.
This is the way I meditate on death.

(*Exit Suwarrow after the Empress.*)

PRINCESS. (*sola.*)

To reason with that butcher, is absurd.
My course, then, is (if possible) to mar
His frightful counsels at the fountain head.
Thus,—while I steer my unsuspected way,
Between the great Dictator and my Spouse
Th' secret medium of communication,—
Here, too, the herald's office I assume
For Lithuania and my nuptial Prince.
In this my twofold character (pray heav'n !)
May honour shield me with unsullied fame !
Nor let that savage rob me of my hopes,
Unceasing as his opposition proves.

So shall I still defy him, still disdain
His cruel malice and corrosive hate,—
Still let him whet his sanguinary fangs,
And gorge on havoc in his blood-stain'd den.
No fear is mine, while *Kosciusko* lives,
And Poland, in *his* valour, *yet survives !*
(*Exit the Princess Lubomirski.*)

(*The Scene changes.*)

ACT III.   SCENE III.

*By moonlight.   In the front a wood.   Near the fore-ground
a castle wall, with a battlemented turret on each side
only partially appearing.   In the centre of the wall is a
grand lofty arched entrance to the court-yard, with
massive gates closed.   In the rear, somewhat remote, a
Castle.*

———

*This Scene commences with a storm of lightning and thunder.
After it subsides, enter the Polish Patriotic Army,
accompanied with pieces of cannon.   Lastly, enter
KOSCIUSKO, in a great state of excitement.*

Kos. (*looking upwards.*)
    Rage on, ye elements,—evince your ire
    At Muscovy's untam'd, perfidious hate!
    Let the whole round of nature's startled hosts
    In one loud burst of indignation roar!
(*To his Army.*)
    Soldiers, here is the Castle where the Court
    Of that arch-demon cumbers the sad earth;—
    Here, too, the prison of my valued friend.
    Returning from th' Crimea, where she left
    Myriads of galling adamantine chains,—
    Th' insatiate tyrant cannot here sojourn
    For a few days, ere her first regal act
    Imprisons my ambassador, and hurls
    Defiance at the laws of God and man.

Blow, then, ye trumpets; let your loudest blast
Rend the afflicted air, and tell that scourge
That we are come, indignant and resolv'd,
Prepar'd to blow her castle to the clouds,
Or rescue the brave partner of our toils!

> (*Several trumpets loudly blow for some minutes.
> Roused by their clangour, Madalinski at
> length appears in chains at the top of one of
> the Towers. Kosciusko recognises him.*)

Is that my friend?—

MAD. 'Tis I,—'tis Madalinski;—hear my chains!

> (*He clanks his chains against the top or battle-
> ments of the Tower.*)

KOS. O shameless outrage! what an act is this!

> (*To some of his Soldiers.*)

Up with the scaling ladders to yon tow'r;—
Lose not a moment till my friend descends.
Blow on, ye trumpets,—let your ceaseless rage
Awake the slumb'rers of that odious den!

> (*While the trumpets are sounding, two scaling
> ladders are accordingly thrown up, so as to
> grapple the battlements of the tower whereon
> Madalinski appears. A Polish soldier
> ascends one of them, and removes the chains
> from the Prisoner. Madalinski, thus libe-
> rated, descends from the tower; after which
> the soldier also comes down. Kosciusko and
> Madalinski embrace. Presently the large
> massive gates are thrown wide open, and
> the Tzarina comes forward, followed by a
> long train densely lined on each side by
> Russian soldiers armed. The Empress
> addresses the Poles in a bold and intrepid
> manner.*)

CATH.   Who dares t' infringe the silence of the night?—

KOS.   A man who dares be honest at *all* times.

CATH.   Your name?

KOS.   My name's a tempest, and my heart a fire;—
My element the stormy track of war.
(Several Russian voices exclaim)
'Tis Kosciusko,—th' great Kosciusko.

CATH.   Kosciusko!

KOS.   You see, great Empress, I am not unknown
Amid your warlike bands;—wherever breathes
A valiant soul among them,—*he* knows *me*.

CATH.   For this nocturnal broil, I must confess,
I should have look'd to any other source.

KOS.   Madam, this nightly broil, as thou *art* pleas'd
To term it, originates not in me;—
It rather springs from perfidy unknown
Except to barb'rous unciviliz'd climes.

CATH.   What, in the name of wonder, is he at?

KOS.   In violation of all human laws,
You seiz'd on my ambassador, and chain'd
Him like a slave;—else you might sleep till midday
Upon your downy pillow undisturb'd.
Nay, you might sleep from day to day, for aught
I wish or care t' interrupt such slumbers
As an *unsleeping* conscience may admit.

CATH.   "Unsleeping conscience!"—Ho! you wish to change
Your military cassock for a *cowl*.
Give up your martial deeds, and I myself
Will make thee my Confess'r :—'tis wonderful
What strange extremes we find in men of parts!

KOS.   Have they who dream of victories and crowns
No vital principle to live beyond
The transient meteors of this desert waste?
Have they *no soul* to wing its way to heav'n,

After they pass like pilgrims thro' this world?
Have they no true or genuine ambition
To live beyond this *span* of human life?—

CATH. Stop, babbling hypocrite!—ambition reigns
In all thy thoughts,—ambition of the worst
And deadliest kind. First, you *dethrone* your king,
And *then* you come to *moralize* with me.

KOS. Excuse me, madam, if in courtesy
I seem deficient, while impell'd to give
A flat denial to the flagrant charge.

CATH. Art thou not Dictator?

KOS. Well, Madam!

CATH. And could you be so, if your sov'reign still
Sat at the helm of his own Monarchy?

KOS. It is admitted that as yet our King
Hath not appear'd unshackled on his throne.
First, *you* enslav'd him; royal Fred'ric next;—
And lastly Austria. To rescue him
From such a hateful state of foreign thraldom,
His patriot subjects have appointed me
To the reluctant office I *now* hold.

CATH. Such is *your* version, where rebellion reigns
And makes a cypher of the very throne.

KOS. Let candid Majesty himself decide.
He *can*, and *will*, declare (if so requir'd)
That he has never felt more truly free,
Than at the present juncture of affairs.

CATH. Yes; you have freed him from Monarchal sway,
And left him leisure to collect his books,
Or mind his aviary, or tune his voice,
Or walk about his garden ev'ry day.
Is this what *you* call liberty?—

KOS. 'Tis its *forerunner*, I sincerely hope.
Yet this is more than Russia's autocrat

G

Would give him by much odds.

CATH. Stop, sir:—did she not raise him to a throne?

Kos. For which we have to thank thee, gen'rous Empress.

CATH. I do not want your thanks;—them I disdain.

Kos. But, if you elevated him so high,—
Thou didst not fail t' keep thy *foot* upon him,
And bid him follow thy *supreme* example.

CATH. Happy idea!—yet the chain, behold,
Of thy great argument, involves thyself.

Kos. How?

CATH. You seem t' insinuate, in treason's speech,
That Stanislas hath trampled on you all.

Kos. No;—I only said, thou bad'st him do so.

CATH. And did he not obey me?

Kos. We ne'er accused him of the foul offence.

CATH. *Then* thou art doubly traitorous and false,
Usurping thy mad office, when your king,
By thine admission, had offended none.

Kos. Nay, madam;—without sophistry I'll solve
Th' enigma in brief space.   After he came,—
(From whatsoever *planet*, save the mark!)
He acted like a Sov'reign much belov'd;—
He nobly gave us a free Constitution,
And prov'd himself the Father of his realm.

CATH. Go on, philosopher, and long remain
In thy well-earn'd dilemma; what came next?

Kos. Need I tell thee,—such a *freeborn* era
Was far *too* much for *tyrants* to behold!—
Hence an unhappy crisis soon arose.

CATH. A most unhappy crisis, past all doubt,
As you and your compatriots shall feel.

Kos. To do thee justice, I must needs confess
No potentate on earth can *threaten* more.

CATH. Ay,—and *fulfil* my promise to the *last*.

Kos.   Mine shall not be *mere language* of defiance;
      Explore the sequel in my future *acts*.   [roar?

Cath. What! would'st thou struggle with the torrent's

Kos.   Yes,—with ten thousand torrents! Where's the
      Or raging cataract, we dread so much   [flood,
      As slavery and chains?

Cath. Rather consider where's the room for hope,
      If Russian, Austrian, and Prussian arms
      Combine against you? what are *you* to stem
      So dire a confluence of armies vast?

Kos.   The willing mind, led on by Providence,
      May hurl a simple sling, and nobly slay
      Th' awful giant of a nation's thraldom.

Cath. Nay,—with my own unaided armaments
      I'd undertake to circumvent you all,
      And blow you like a vapour out of being.

Kos.   Madam, believe me, you may strive to drown
      The monitor within you for awhile;
      But *yet*, its awful warnings will be heard;—
      Still will the sighs of immortality
      Assert their pow'r, tho' dismal silence long
      May (as it were) seal up their *still small voice;* —
      The time approaches when their period comes,—
      No more to *whisper* in our list'ning ears,
      But with *the loudest thunders to awake*
      The noblest dreamer of the present scene.

Cath. Doubtless, thou wert intended for a priest,
      Or holy friar,—Dominican or grey,—
      Franciscan, Jesuit, or Jansenist.
      Let me, then, hear thy lecture to its close;—
      Go on, Confessor,—military monk,—
      Fancy you *now* address some erring nun,
      And do thy function with a manly grace.
        (*Here the Empress Catherine endeavours to*

*force a smile expressive of contempt as well
as levity.*)

Kos. Hah! canst thou smile, as if no pang within
Lay rankling in thy fluctuating breast?
Can you still smile at your ensanguin'd course
That holds a sceptre o'er a sea of woe?
Can you smile *always?* Can you smile at *death?*
Or can you smile at *that,* O mighty Queen?
*(While asking this last question, he appears
greatly moved or agitated.)*

Cath. At what?! (*in a very enquiring manner.*)

Kos. At that pale Vision of the troubled night!—
It seems to wear a crown;—*now* shows its wounds;—
Now points to thee;—now tumbles from a *throne.*
Dost thou not see it? is it possible?—
Lo! *now* it closer moves, as if to soothe
The palpitation of a Royal Spouse!
O heav'ns! it seems prepar'd to grasp thee round,
To fold thee in its shrouds, and take thee hence.
*(Here Catherine shrieks, and becomes terribly
alarmed.)*

Spirit of whatever region, what disturbs
Thy mist-like form?—Ha! do thy wounds begin
To bleed afresh?—they spout like salient streams;—
On all her royal robes the crimson flood
Appears to issue with relentless sway.
Oh! what an awful sight!—she's bath'd in blood,
Ev'n in a husband's blood, from head to foot.
*(Here Catherine sinks down, partially supported
by two of her maids of honour. Great con-
sternation pervades all present, while an
indistinct luminous appearance crosses the
entire Stage a few feet distant from the floor.
The Vision has no regularly defined form,*

*but seems like a collection of regal habili-
ments (stained with blood) somewhat similar
to thin luminous clouds or mists. This is
merely intended to delineate to the audience
the apparition which Catherine, thus wrought
on, fancied she actually saw. Lightnings
and thunderings again come on. At the
first intermission of these tempestuous accom-
paniments, Kosciusko gives a motion with
his hand, in obedience to which the trumpet
sounds the signal of recal.*

*Exeunt Kosciusko and Madalinski, in a very
slow and solemn mood, the* former *leaning
on the arm of the* latter, *followed by all the
Poles and their Artillery; while the Russians
stand looking on, in silent stupor and amazement.*)

(*Here the Curtain drops.*)

END OF THE THIRD ACT.

ACT IV.　Scene I.

A wood; in the rear of which, are some trunks of felled
Timber.

———

This Scene commences with a confused clangour of trumpets
heard from various directions: also heavy Parks of
Artillery are heard firing at a distance. Finally the
trumpet of retreat is sounded; and three successive bodies
of Prussians, at short intervals, rush across the Stage
driven before the victorious Poles.

Enter FREDERIC, *precipitately followed by* KOSCIUSKO;
both with drawn swords.

Kos.　　Hah! have we met at length, O King?
FRED.　　True, Kosciusko,—but 'tis out of place;—
　　　　So there remain, with all your merry men,
　　　　Till my return;—I'll come again, you'll find.
　　　　　　(*Exit Frederic with a train of followers just*
　　　　　　　come up.
　　　　　　　Enter a Polish soldier with a letter, which he
　　　　　　　gives to the Dictator, and immediately Exits.)
　(*A voice without.*)
　　　　Th' foe is coming fast in this direction.
Kos.　　Meet them, then;—sound the charge; let ev'ry
　　　　Dash onward at them like electric fire.　　[man
　　　　Tell them, I dispute that pass; show them *there*

A wall of Polish spears, while I peruse
This letter; tow'rds the river glance them off.
(*He reads as follows :—*)

> " My dear Friend,—I have to inform your
> Excellency,—unaccountable as it might other-
> wise appear,—that *forty thousand* Prussians
> have been put to flight. The whole difficulty
> is now completely solved, as intelligence hath
> arrived of various insurrections in the Polish
> Provinces recently annexed to Prussia. The
> Prussian yoke there is extremely galling. In
> all his new provinces Frederic William hath
> introduced German laws, and has even gone so
> far as to oblige his vanquished subjects to
> learn the language of their victors. Our coun-
> trymen accordingly foresee that, in those re-
> gions, it is manifestly intended to eradicate
> everything Polish from the face of the earth.
> This news I have obtained from Despatches
> which a Courier of the enemy dropped in the
> confusion of their *retreat*, and may be relied on
> as undoubtedly authentic.
> " Yours as ever, &c. &c. &c.
> " DOMBROWSKI."

This is most fortunate! with such a chasm
As the retreat of forty thousand men
So opportunely makes on th' adverse side,—
Our course at length in one bright current runs.
Henceforth, with undivided armaments,
We'll teach the fell Suwarrow to suspect
That he is not invincible, tho' flush'd
With victories obtain'd in Turkish realms.
But hold,—I've been so long unvisited

By soothing sleep in this untir'd campaign,—
I dare not quarrel with her present summons.
Yet where's her pillow and her welcome couch?
                              (*He looks round.*)
Ha! there I see it! 'tis a sylvan bed,
And soft enough for any true-bred soldier.
The battle also slumbers;—so shall I.

> (*He retires, and lies down on one of the trunks
> of the felled trees, having his head on another
> trunk which happens to be more elevated.
> Here he has a most remarkable Dream, which
> is prefigured by a succession of Images in
> Luminous Clouds. A Heavenly Choir is
> heard (not seen) singing throughout this
> aërial preintimation of* future events.)

1st. A GLEE, *by either* 3 *or* 4 *voices.*

Favour'd of heav'n, receive
What happy angels give;—
For, where in sleep no guilty thunders roll,
With pleasing visions we delight the soul.
Such is virtue's sov'reign pow'r,
Heav'nly rays sublime her views,
Ev'n in danger's cloud-cast hour
Yielding hope in all her hues.

2ndly. A PROPHETIC SOLO, *Recitative.*

Sometimes the deer escapes,—sometimes he dies;—
Man, like the deer, oft hears the hunter's cries.
Tumult on tumult,—such is Heav'n's decree,
Joy follows joy, before the soul is free.

3rdly. Partly as a DUET, *and partly as a* TRIO *or* CHORUS.

Heav'n is just in all her ways,
Hence her voice whoe'er obeys—
Meets with ruin never ;
For, on earth tho' virtue sighs,
Soon she journeys to the skies,
There to reign for ever.

> (*While the above Stanzas are sung, there is a
> constant succession of Mystic Scenes in
> beautifully diversified Clouds, emblematic of
> various changes in States and Empires.
> Among these misty prefigurations of coming
> events, the following are not the least
> remarkable. Another* PARTITIONING OF
> POLAND *is thus represented:—There is a
> large splendid vestment in various colours,
> worn by a very interesting female, over whose
> head is inscribed, in transparent characters,
> the word "*POLAND.*" Three other female
> figures lay violent hands on this attractive
> vesture, and rend it into* three *portions,
> each retaining a large part for herself.
> These Three have the words "*RUSSIA,*"
> "*PRUSSIA,*" and "*AUSTRIA*" respectively
> written over their heads. They bear away
> the Prize, and "*POLAND*" follows them in
> a supplicating posture. This is one of the
> Visions of the Dream.*
> *Another Vision is as follows:—There is a
> very great excitement among a group of
> female figures, over whose heads, in similar
> transparent characters, are respectively in-*

scribed the names of the great nations of
EUROPE. They all cast a very attentive eye
on "POLAND," who (at one time) is represented as gradually sinking down, lower and
lower, till at length she becomes entirely
prostrate. At this crisis, four female
figures go to her assistance, and gradually
raise her up. Over their heads are written
"BRITANNIA," "GALLIA," "HIBERNIA,"
and "SCOTIA."

Another Vision is thus represented:—Three
female figures appear, having respectively
written over their heads — "RUSSIA,"
"TURKEY," and "INDIA." Russia seizes
Turkey and lays her prostrate beneath her;
and, on the other side, lays hold of one of
the garments of India. At this juncture
Britannia (with a lion couching at her foot,
and looking furiously at Russia) rescues the
Garment of India out of her hand, and
drives her away. Thus Russia flies from
the pursuing Britannia, accompanied by the
lion now rampant and raging after the
fugitive Autocrat.

The Three Visions, here set forth, may serve
as a specimen of a numerous train of similar
preintimations of FUTURE EVENTS, which
abound throughout this most SIGNIFICANT
DREAM.

The series of Luminous Clouds at length
terminates, and Kosciusko awakes out of
sleep. He rises from the trunks of the
felled trees, whereon he had slept, and comes
forward in a very thoughtful mood.)

Kos. (*solus.*)

Think, as ye will, of dreams,—insane mankind,
They fail not to evince, past ev'ry doubt,
A sep'rate and peculiar energy
Of purely mental birth,—where in the soul
Th' scenes of life recur, unclogg'd by matter,
Gliding alone on intellectual wing.
Nor, in this instance, is their airy world
To *past events* confin'd;—witness the voice
Prophetic that pervades these mental flights.

(*Looking to one side.*)

Yet who comes here,—to interrupt my thoughts
On this *momentous vision?*—heav'nly pow'rs
Forgive my present flight! when time permits,
In contemplation we shall meet again.

Enter MADALINSKI.

What now, my friend?
MADAL. My Lord Dictator, I come overwhelm'd
With most disastrous news.
Kos. Quickly unfold it,—let it blow what will!
MADAL. Chrysillida and Radziwilla both
Are pris'ners of Suwarrow.
Kos. O cruel destiny! But tell me where
Their consorts are? I fear they're fall'n in battle.
MADAL. My information, I regret to state,
Is silent on that subject;—what I heard,
I panted to communicate in haste;
Hence I delay'd not to explore the rest.
Kos. Well, well! no time is to be lost;—come on.
(*Exeunt; Kosciusko going first.*)

(*The Scene changes.*)

ACT IV.   Scene II.

Another wood, of deep perspective.

———

*This Scene opens with Radziwilla reclining over the body of
Kollontay, and Chrysillida over that of Dzialinski, in
the rear ground ; both their husbands having been slain
in battle.*

Here also is Suwarrow, *with Russian forces on each side.*

Suwar. (*coming forward.*)
 So ho! my pretty birds are cag'd at last.
 Ferzen, I ween, with all his fine tirades,
 Would not be loth t'admire their beauteous crest.
 But *neither* shall be his ;—I'll take them both
 Under my own peculiar patronage,
 And try to *woo* them like a lover true.
 Turkey's the land where beauteous women hail
 A Russian conqueror with open arms.
 These, I suspect, will act a diff'rent part;—
 But I shall follow them, where'er they go.
 Despair had almost seiz'd me ;—I began
 To think we never could secure them living,—
 They fought with such dexterity and fire :—
 But, since their husbands fell, in grief o'erwhelm'd
 They seem almost unconscious they're our pris'ners

(Here he turns round, and moves towards the rear in a very slow pace. While Suwarrow is retiring, a trumpet, without, loudly sounds to the charge. Astonishment seizes the Russians: presently Enter KOSCIUSKO *with sword in hand, followed by a chosen band of Poles with Madalinski at their head.)*

SUWAR. *(drawing his sword.)*
Hail, Kosciusko! I'm glad to see thee.

KOS. Receive, then, my salute;—'tis quite in point.
(They engage each other with very great animation. While they are warmly contesting, Madalinski's party, in a most furious onset, expel the Russians, and Exeunt *driving them on before them. Lastly, in the same direction,* Exeunt *Suwarrow and Kosciusko still fighting; the former being driven on by the latter. Meanwhile, Radsiwilla and Chrysillida, roused by the tumult, and having left the bodies of their slain consorts, come forward, still gazing with vast amazement, and looking now towards one side.)*

CHRY. Oh! my dear Sister! what is this we see?

RADZ. The noble Kosciusko, I believe,
Hath routed that infernal Muscovite.

CHRY. Yes;—I begin to think so;—mem'ry seems
Returning on me;—O my harrow'd soul!
Yet, Radziwilla, where is now the use
Of fighting for so desolate a pair?

RADZ. I hope our friend has kill'd him.

CHRY. 'Twould do a service to mankind.

RADZ. Lo, th' enemy is fled, but not despatch'd.

CHRY. A day there was, when we would not look on
In such a state of listless indolence.

H

Re-enter KOSCIUSKO.

Kos.   Dearest of friends,—how greatly I rejoice
        To see you rescued from so dire a scourge!
CHRY.   Noble Dictator, well as we can thank you   .
        Call us grateful! yet what is life to *us*,
        Reft as we are of consorts so belov'd?
        Ah! Kosciusko, we are *widows now*;—
        The nuptial mantle that for many years   .
        So kindly shelter'd us from ev'ry storm,
        Is now remov'd and violently rent,
        And prostrate on the earth before thee lies.
            (*Here she points to the dead bodies of their
            husbands.*)
        Yes; look on *them*, and tell us what *we* are.
RADZ.   Oh, what a wreck is now before our eyes!
        The awful visitation rolls around,—
        While from our breasts dissever'd, sadly torn,
        Th' beings, in whom we liv'd, are gone for ever!
        No more to hail us with th' ecstatic throb
        Of sweet affection and the purest love:—
        No more to take our children on their knee,
        And give them the rever'd paternal kiss:—
        No more to bless our dwellings with their smiles;—
        No; but to mingle with their parent dust.
CHRY.   Surely this state of our existence seems
        A *rueful* vista to another world.
        Come, then, what will,—I cannot deeper plunge
        Into the lap of human misery.
        Why have I liv'd to witness such an hour?
RADZ.   Ah! wherefore was *I* born?
CHRY.   'Tis vain to struggle any longer here;
        O my soul, go on! cast off all your fetters!

Burst the sad tenement that chains thee down!
Force, force your way! nor ever let your course
Be stopp'd on this side of the ruthless grave;—
Till from your mortal prison you ascend
Into your own immortal empire,—there—
Yes *there*—(Heav'n grant!) to join our friends again
With better auspices and brighter hopes!
> (*Here Radziwilla clasps Chrysillida in her
> arms; and both remain firmly folded in each
> other's embrace for some time. Kosciusko
> slowly moves forward in great grief.*)

Kos. (*to himself.*)

Oft have I trod th' ensanguin'd plains of war,
And known vicissitudes in ev'ry form;—
But till this moment I could never say
That real agony assail'd my soul.
O Kosciusko, thou hast lost in them
Two valued friends as ever breath'd on earth!
The widows and the orphans they have left—
O heav'ns! it is a direful piteous sight!
I never knew perplexity before.
Untutor'd in the school of nuptial life,
I know not how to vent my *lab'ring* mind;—
Nor have I ever seen the least success
Attend officious counsel, at a time
When human nature with excessive grief
Was bursting into madness and despair.
Short, then, be my attempt at consolation.

(*To them.*)

Ladies, most valued of your sex, receive
From me a tributary tear! Behold
How much devolves on me! that same increas'd—
Most poignantly increas'd by the sad cause
Of your profound affliction and my own!

Excuse me, then, by duty thus impell'd
To *guard you* still, as well as *guide* the *helm ;—*
I must away ; but, ere I go, I'll leave you
To a far better care-taker—to Heav'n !
Adieu, my friends ! our parting is, I trust,
No more than momentary : (*aside*) tho', perhaps,
It is a solemn, long, and last farewell !
  (*Exit Kosciusko slowly, and altogether like a*
  man struggling with his feelings.

(*The Scene immediately changes.*)

ACT IV. Scene III.

An apartment, looking into a back lawn, and having in its centre a lofty arch with folding doors open.

———

Enter Frederic.

Fred. (*solus.*)

So Stanislas hath quarrell'd with his friend;—
Like a high-mettled charger off he goes.
'Tis not his first attempt;—nor shall it be,
If I have any wit, his final plunge.
I'll try to lure him back,—and train him better.
Meanwhile we must be stirring, since these dogs,
These Polish dogs of ours have ceas'd to bite.

> (*Turning about, and addressing his Army,
> part whereof now appear, through the cen-
> tral arch, in the lawn in the rear.*)

Let the loud trumpet sound an instant charge!
We'll show those patriots how well we rally.

> (*The Prussian trumpet,* without, *sounds as
> directed.*)

Now let th' van proceed;—I'll shortly follow.

> (*The van of the Prussian Army march on out-
> side, cross the central arch, and so Exeunt
> in the rear.*)

Should th' war take a southward line of action,
I'll place the enemy between two fires.

H 2

This I'll effect by certain signal rockets,
Like telegraphic characters arrang'd.
Obedient to this novel stratagem
An overwhelming armament shall move,
And, under cover of th' unconscious night,
Shall give those patriots a warm embrace.
This, too, occurring where they least suspect,
Will so astound the circumvented foe,
That (if *my* augury may prove correct),
'Twill shortly end this obstinate campaign.
Poor devils! how they'll writhe beneath the show'rs
Which our artillery shall pour upon them!
Nay; it is e'en a source of grief to me,
To have recourse to such an awful scourge.
           (*Exit Frederic through the archway.*)

        (*The Scene changes.*)

ACT IV. SCENE IV.

A wood, with a drop-scene which represents a country in long or deep perspective.

———

Enter MADALINSKI.

MADAL. (*solus.*)
That vile Poninski I could never trust;
I always felt disdain 'neath his command.
Would we had known him sooner! wisdom thus
Too often lags behind the traitor's lunge.
But yonder Kosciusko, like the wind,
Carries a tempest in his ev'ry look.
How shall I meet him?—how communicate
The sad disaster which portends our ruin?

Enter KOSCIUSKO, in great haste.

KOS.   My friend, I'm glad to meet thee at this crisis.
The army of Suwarrow hath been kept
Completely separate from Ferzen's force:
Had they but join'd,—our enterprise had fail'd.
But what is this I witness in thy looks,
Now that the Prussians have resum'd the war?
A cloud on battle's ardent mien conveys
More than a volume!—Madalinski, speak!
MADAL. What valour could perform was nobly done,

And all appear'd to promise great results ;—
But what the honest course of conquest fail'd
To give our enemy,—may yet be done
By treason's undermining influence.

Kos. (*astonished.*)
Explain thyself!

MADAL. Poninski is a traitor,—he whose bands
Were now expected in this very point.

Kos. Ha! is it possible?—Poninski!

MADAL. The foe advances fast; but where great strength
Was doubly wanting, weakness only reigns,—
All owing to that demon of deception.

Kos. The dastard coward! who could choose to raise
A heap of gold upon his Country's ruin!
Paltry equivalent for all that springs
From ignominy's false and perjur'd train!—
Where are the forces whom the traitor led?

MADAL. By varied artifice and foul deceit,
Against their own conviction, he allur'd
The greater portion into deep defiles,
As if for preconcerted ambuscades.
Thence (as it were), lock'd in by hostile hordes,
'Tis easy to infer the sequel dire.

Kos. Wert thou a witness of the fatal scene?

MADAL. Alas! *too true!* but with a world of toil
My troops surmounted e'en this adverse stroke,
Cutting an awful vista through the foe.

Kos. Brave fellows! worthy of a better lot
Than following that base abandon'd wretch!
Yet what is to be done? no time is ours
To waste away in indolent regret.

MADAL. We're all agreed, and only wait for thee
To sanction or reject what we advise.

Kos. Say on.

MADAL. With mighty effort let us sally forth
   Into the thickest of the hostile ranks,—
   Prepar'd (if possible) to turn the scale,
   Or die with honour in the great attempt.

KOS. 'Tis nobly said; I like the bold device;—
   Yes, it is well conceiv'd, whate'er betide.
   Come, then, brave comrade, like a storm on fire
   To howl o'er desolation might and main.

MADAL. Not so, great Captain, if our will prevail.
   Leave *us* to perish,—but let Poland still
   Preserve her best, her only guardian hope!

KOS. And dost thou think to leave your chief behind,
   To mourn, like woman, o'er th' tombs of heroes?
   Never, Oh never, while this arm can wield
   My trusty sword in Poland's proud defence.

MADAL. Consider, Kosciusko, if *we* fall,
   We scarcely can be miss'd, while *thou* remain'st;
   But if thy vital lamp should chance t' expire,
   Our Country's fun'ral knell must soon succeed.

KOS. Pshaw! never mention it;—name it no more;—
   The very thought inflicts a deeper wound
   Than all our enemies could ever give.
   No; let me fall in glory's vast career,—
   If so it *must* be,—let me fall at once;—
   Let me share also ev'ry scar with *you;*—
   To *die* in such a cause is *life* itself.
   Come, then, companion dear; tho' it may seem
   No better than a *desp'rate forlorn hope!*
   Since all are resolute, let's plough our way
   Thro' yon advancing column of the foe!
     (*Exeunt Kosciusko and Madalinski.*)

(*The Scene changes.*)

ACT IV. SCENE V.

*Another wood, with a large cross range of rocks beautifully
diversified with shrubs, and clothed with autumnal foliage.*

———

First, *This Scene commences with a band of music heard
playing as from a distance.*
Secondly, *A distant cannonade is heard like slow rumbling
of remote thunder for some time.*
Thirdly, *A Polish Bugle sounds to the charge without, at
one side.*
Fourthly, *It is presently answered by a Russian trumpet,
without, at the other side.*
Fifthly, *Enter* MADALINSKI, *leading on a body of resolute
Polish Troops. He looks toward one side, without intermission, during his following address to his soldiers.*

MADAL. Oh, how unfortunate it is to be
        Thus separated from our martial Chief!
        The floods of war were irresistible;—
        They cut our columns into num'rous parts.
        Yonder another hostile deluge rolls;—
        Onward it rages with tremendous strides.
        Lo! *there* th' unaw'd Dictator reappears
        Plowing his stormy way thro' myriads fall'n!
        On, on, ye brave;—a resolute advance
        May reunite our forces and prevail.

Stop not your furious onset till you blot
Your Country's foes completely out of being!

> (*Exeunt all briskly; Madalinski going first.
> Without, after a few seconds' lapse, there
> is a great clashing of swords, succeeded by a
> vast tumult, which soon dies away. Pre-
> sently, for a short time, as if in commemo-
> ration of victory, a band of music is heard
> playing. It ceases,*)

(*And the Scene changes.*)

ACT IV.　Scene VI.

A wood, with a tolerably elevated table-land, at one side, running far back in the rear, and extending near the front. There is also a small portion of similarly elevated table-land, at the other side, far back in the rear. A rustic bridge there rests on the two table-lands. A river winds along the base of the greater table-land, and flows out of view, after passing under the bridge. On this, the greater table-land, are placed two biers (side by side, in close contact, and having their ends visible), with the Corses of Kollontay and Dzialinski, each covered with a black velvet pall, under a canopy, like a tent with curtains thrown wide open. There Radziwilla and Chrysillida appear respectively reclining on their slain husbands.

Below, *near the front, in the centre, on a rising knoll about two feet from the floor,* Kosciusko *reclines on his arm, with sword in hand, surrounded by the bodies of his slain friends, viz. that of Madalinski, and several others.*

Kos.　Have I been slumb'ring long amid the dead—
Surrounded by my friends—who bravely fought
Till cover'd like myself with countless wounds?
Are they still bleeding on the parent soil?—
Say, Mokranowski, has thy spirit fled?—
Or thine, Dombrowski, valour's far-fam'd son?—

Oginski !—Dzialinski !—Kollontay !—
Ah ! these are surely number'd with the dead !
Zajonezec, art thou silent, too ?—or thou,
Heroic Madalinski, honour'd friend,.
Whose heart with mine would shed its latest drop
Upon the altar of thy native land ?—
Is there no tongue,—no voice to answer me ?
Are all as mute as Nature's speechless grave ?
Then let *me* die !—I've been too long on earth
To witness such an awful stillness here.

Enter FERZEN, *the Russian General, accompanied by some of his soldiers. One of them, perceiving Kosciusko sitting up and leaning on his sword, goes towards him, and is about to run him through with his fixed bayonet.*

FERZEN (*preventing him.*)
        What ! would'st thou kill Kosciusko ?
                (*The Soldier, surprised, desists from his pur-
                pose, and lets his firelock fall to the ground.
                Mute astonishment seizes the Russians.*)
Kos.   Ay, let him strike ! my country hath receiv'd
        A greater blow ;—I wish not to survive
        The fatal hour when Poland clanks her chains !
FERZEN (*to his soldiers.*)
        Warfare hath done its part ; henceforth in peace
        Behold yon prostrate hero ! (*aside.*) I'm inclin'd
        To go myself and seek some skilful surgeon.
        To see th' brave and matchless Kosciusko
        In such a situation, chills my soul.
        Come, soldiers, follow.
                (*Exit Ferzen, followed by his soldiers.*)
Kos. (*to himself.*)
        Victor and Vanquish'd, too, seem *both* alike.

                        I

The *former*, tho' triumphant, is a slave ;—
The *latter* is no more,—tho' nobly led,
Aspiring after liberty,—to fall.
O death ! thy sceptre is upon me !—hah !

(*Kosciusko ceases to recline, now falling completely prostrate. In this situation he continues silent and motionless for a long time.*

Above, *Enter a party of Russians, who cross
over the rustic bridge, and immediately on
the other side encounter (sword in hand) the
Poles stationed there, on the main table-land,
as a guard to the heroic and disconsolate
widows. These, after an obstinate resistance, are routed, and* Exeunt *on that
table-land Meanwhile,* RADZIWILLA *and*
CHRYSILLIDA, *roused by this contest, had
abandoned their inclined position over their
husbands' corses, had drawn their swords,
and had sternly viewed this Engagement, to
them so ultimately adverse.*)

CHRY.   Others may fly ; but on this sacred spot
           Let's sell our lives as dearly as we can !
RADZ.   Yes, and avenge our consorts' cruel death !
CHRY.   'Tis our best safeguard,—while affrighted virtue
           Anticipates no mercy at their hands.
A RUSSIAN. Yield yourselves instant pris'ners, or you die.
RADZ.   What ? do you dare to threaten *us* with death,—
           We, who disdain existence unreveng'd !
CHRY.   No ; we shall never yield ;—no parley we
           Desire from such a sanguinary foe !
A RUSSIAN. Change your minds instantly, or dread our pow'r.
RADZ.   Come on, dear sister ; let's engage at once !

(*They both dash at the Russians with vast
resolution, sword in hand ; and the* latter

*retreat precipitately over the bridge. Just
as they reach the bridge, the two widows
pause, and return from the pursuit to their
former position.)*

CHRY. 'Tis a mere feint;—they merely wish to draw
Us from our Citadel, as this shall be.

RADZ. That were a vain attempt, if I can judge
Of your determination and my own.

CHRY. We'll follow them no more, but here abide
To end our pilgrimage in honour's cause.

RADZ. It is the utmost we can hope to gain,
A happy liberation out of woe.

*(Re-enter the Russians, crossing the bridge
again, and proceeding with cautious steps.)*

CHRY. Lo! they return;—insidiously they come.
Be guarded, Sister, or the tigers' bound
May take us by surprise and force us off.

RADZ. Never, Chrysillida, while thus resolv'd
To wield our trusty falchions to the last.

CHRY. Come on, ye wolves; your prey is *now* prepar'd;
But you must kill it ere you call it yours.

A RUSSIAN. On, Russians, on; 'tis vain to loiter more.

*(They now make many fruitless attempts to
take the two heroic widows alive; so dex-
terously do the latter parry off every ap-
proach, while numbers of the Enemy are
slain by them.)*

A RUSSIAN. We're losing many lives.

ANOTHER. Then let us kill them, or they'll kill us all.

*(The Russians now press onward in a body,
and run both Radziwilla and Chrysillida
through with their swords.)*

RADZ. I'm dying, dearest-Sister!

CURY. So am I : kind Heav'n be prais'd!

> (*Their swords drop from their hands ; they
> fall down beside their husbands' bier and
> expire.*
>
> *Re-enter the Poles, rallying on the main table-
> land. They soon put the Russians to flight,
> who retreat precipitately over the rustic
> bridge. The victors continue the pursuit ;
> thus all Exeunt there.*
>
> *Next, Enter two Polish women, who draw the
> curtains of the tent (on the main table-land)
> quite close ; hence all there become invisible
> to the End.*
>
> *Re-enter,* below, FERZEN *with his back turned
> towards the Dictator. The* latter *now
> seems like a person roused out of a reverie ;
> he rises to his former reclining position.*)

KOS. I think I heard the distant clash of arms ;—
But lo ! who is that Russian General?

FERZEN (*turning round.*)
'Tis I, illustrious Chieftain, just return'd,—
A surgeon is expected ev'ry moment.

KOS. Ferzen, I'm glad it's *you ;* I hate so much
The dire Suwarrow, that most cruel scourge
Who lately gave our city to the flames :
Nor age, nor virtue, sanctity, nor sex,
Nor aught appearing like humanity,
Could for a moment stay the brutal rage
That left all Cracow in one mass of ruin.

FERZEN (*aside.*)
This is a subject I must wisely shun.

(*To him.*)Mighty, tho' fallen, Chieftain, could'st thou bear
Removal in thy present feeble state ?

Kos.   My body's like a target riddled o'er   [flowing,
       With num'rous wounds :—th' streams of life are
       Not as before,—but to manure the earth.
       Mind not the prostrate Kosciusko, then;
       Far other cares are crowding in his thoughts.
       Have any tidings reach'd thine ear of late,
       Of Radziwilla and Chrysillida?

Ferzen. Not a syllable.

Kos.   Oh dire suspense! tho' why presume to hope
       Those patriotic widows could survive
       A period so replete with Poland's wrongs?
       Their hearts would break, if conscious of the ruin
       Which ev'rywhere around their country rolls.
       But, if they live; in honour let them live ;—
       I say, brave General,—in *honour live*
       Far from that odious demon of the north,
       The fell Suwarrow, who nor God nor man
       Regards,—but, like a pestilential blast,
       Moves o'er creation with a fury's howl:—
       Save them from *him*, and be for ever bless'd!

Ferzen. Far as my influence extends, I promise.

Kos.   Make me *one* other promise, and I've done.
       Since morn arose, Oh tell me, hast thou seen
       The Princess Lubomirski and her son?

Ferzen. They're both our pris'ners, and will soon be here.

Kos.   Why your *pris'ners?* Sure, they are not like *me*,
       Your steadfast enemy : what have *they* done?

Ferzen. The youth seem'd bent on mischief; but we soon
       Begirt him round, and took away his sword.

Kos.   Poh! he's a boy,—a mere, mere boy.

Ferzen. Egad, an army of such very boys
       Would keep us all a-stirring right and left.

Kos.   His gen'rous mother came on embassy
       To your proud Empress,—and as such demands

A passport to her long-absented home.

FERZEN. That she was offer'd, but without her son
Prefers captivity,—or even death.

Kos. And wouldst thou take away her only joy,—
The only male companion of her course?—
Surely thou wilt not,—if a Soldier's honour
Can prove a barrier to th' inglorious deed.
Shall Kosciusko plead for them in vain,—
That prostrate enemy who gave you all
Enough to do, as long as he could stand?
Now that he lingers on his mother earth,—
Perhaps, ere night, to yield his vital spark
To that dear Country where he first drew breath,—
Wilt thou deny him *this*—his *last* request?

> (*Here Ferzen, previously agitated, clasps his
> hands, and appears deeply affected. The
> attention of all is suddenly arrested by a
> confused clangour of trumpets, without,
> and the crowding in of Russian Soldiers,
> who enter from all directions with Polish
> Captives, male and female. Next the
> Princess Lubomirski and her son are led in;
> the latter being in chains. At seeing
> Kosciusko in his reclining and wounded
> state, she shrieks and falls on the shoulders
> of her equally-sorrowing son the young
> Prince Charles. In this afflicting posture
> of affairs, the Curtain drops, ending the
> Drama.*)

THE END.

WILSON AND OGILVY, SKINNER STREET, LONDON.

Lightning Source UK Ltd.
Milton Keynes UK
UKOW051828281012

201323UK00015B/56/P